MOMS

— FOR —

HIRE

MOMS

— FOR —

HIRE

8 STEPS TO KICKSTART YOUR NEXT CAREER

DEBORAH JELIN NEWMYER

FOREWORD BY KATHLEEN KENNEDY

Skyhorse Publishing

Skyhorse Publishing books may be purchased in bulk at special discounts for sales promotion, corporate gifts, fund-raising, or educational purposes. Special editions can also be created to specifications. For details, contact the Special Sales Department, Skyhorse Publishing, 307 West 36th Street, 11th Floor, New York, NY 10018 or info@skyhorsepublishing.com.

Skyhorse® and Skyhorse Publishing® are registered trademarks of Skyhorse Publishing, Inc.®, a Delaware corporation.

Visit our website at www.skyhorsepublishing.com.

10 9 8 7 6 5 4 3 2 1

Library of Congress Cataloging-in-Publication Data is available on file.

Cover design by Jenny Zemanek
Cover photo credit: iStock

Print ISBN: 978-1-5107-0569-2
Ebook ISBN: 978-1-5107-0570-8

Printed in China

Dedicated to Every Mom—
Past, Present, and Future

Especially my Mom,
Sima Kislak Jelin
. . . my first and favorite bossy girlfriend

CONTENTS

FOREWORD

I met Deb when she was a gangly, idealistic twenty-something, applying for a job at Amblin Entertainment. We were a small production company with ten full-time employees in the middle of producing *The Goonies*, and we needed some fresh voices and enthusiastic hands to help out.

In her first interview, Deb seemed to have the skills and stamina for the job, but she separated herself from the pack with her common sense opinions and her unabashed candor. I valued her boldness and introduced her to Steven Spielberg, and, without a hint of nervousness, she pitched out her favorite scenes from the novel *The Color Purple,* emphasizing a few moments that felt especially cinematic. She got the job. And Steven made the movie.

We worked closely together as a team for the next thirteen years. Everybody flourished, and Deb grew with the company to become senior executive and executive producer on several films, including *Little Rascals, An American Tail, Land Before Time,* and *How to Make an American Quilt.*

Since then, I have watched Deb indomitably reinvent herself many times—from a young go-getter, to a working mother with a few babies, to a freelance independent producer, to suddenly a widowed mother of four, who then circled back into the workforce with verve and conviction to produce films and the hit TV series *The Sing-Off.*

Throughout the decades of ups-and-downs, Deb always brought along the laughs. Never cynical or at someone else's expense, Deb wore lenses that saw the funny zing in most things, whether it is a complex movie idea, a kid's dilemma, or a friend's struggle. Her rose-colored bounce could turn those long working hours into a joyous experience.

I will never forget when we would skip lunch to jog around Toluca Lake and reboot ourselves. On one such autumn run, a pinecone was in Deb's path, and she went down. Her ankle was twisted, but we were a mile from the office. Deb got up, limped a little, and quoted her mom: "Walk it off . . . it will be better in the morning." We slowed a bit, Deb grimaced, but onward we went. Turned out it was a pretty bad sprain. Doctors, X-rays, and crutches followed. But Deb never complained. She kept that foot elevated, and somehow, we laughed. Her only request was that on my next solo run, I'd look for that offending pinecone. She wanted to use it as a paperweight to remind her to always "Walk it off . . . it will be better in the morning."

I know that whatever orbit Deb chooses, she will succeed. Through tragedy or glory, she always remains present and true. I look forward to our catch-up dinners and adventures. I can count on real laughter, honest tears, and everlasting insights.

In writing *Moms for Hire,* Deb has essentially written the book *Lean **Back** In*—an appealing and indispensable manual for any woman who wants to reenter the working world. She has succeeded in so many facets of work and parenting to become an expert herself in this debate. No one can gently boss people around or help them navigate (and then defuse) the minefields of a mom's daily struggles better than my friend and colleague, Deborah Jelin Newmyer.

So . . . Listen to Deb. I know I do.

Kathleen Kennedy started her career, while still in college, as a camera operator at her local San Diego television station. The first movie she produced was ET *(1982), and she continued to produce over 60 films including* Raiders of the Lost Ark, The Color Purple, Jurassic Park, *and* Schindler's List. *In 2012, Kathy became president of Lucasfilm and reinvigorated the Star Wars franchise. She is married to fellow producer Frank Marshall, and when not on a far-off production set, they live in Los Angeles with their two teenaged daughters.*

THE INTRO

Growing up, we all dreamed of becoming some sort of princess. My princess was going to live in a Technicolor world. . . . Not as a damsel in distress. Not laden with a weighty crown. Or twisted up in a superhero cape. Nope. My princess plan was to be a sharp-witted, tough-willed, respected, and beloved ruler of a 3-D castle on the hill. I would be adored by fine children and a dashing husband. My princess was going to have her name in lights for curing real things and brokering real peace. Dragons would meet their match. And, of course, I would have great hair.

And then, there was a honk.

It was 2:55 p.m. My dusty Toyota hybrid was silently waiting in the carpool pickup lane behind several minivans. That day I had proudly completed the crossword puzzle but couldn't claim any other significant accomplishment since dropping off my third grader at school six hours earlier.

The irony was not lost on me that the first question I would ask my sweet, sweaty-faced child was:

"Hey, Hon! So what did you do today?"

Oh how I hoped nobody would ask me that very same question.

Once, I could so casually brag about my workday. It was filled with power meetings, bustling ideas, and designer-ish suits. I was speed-dialing top agents and talent, and I was respected and invited inside for my producing skills. That snapshot of sassy careerist has turned in dress and in attitude. That castle on a hilltop had moved far far away. And out of the front window, all I could see were moats and gatekeepers.

I was still the same Deb: energetic, bossy, and likeable, but somehow in the mulch of skating schedules and separated socks, I was cheering on the sidelines, doling out perfect orange wedges, fostering someone else's signature. When the passport office asked me to write down my occupation, I was stumped.

I had always been a book browser, so I went foraging for a guidebook to help me reignite my professional mojo. Books had always given me answers, and provided me decades of information and pleasure. Books had insulated every home—they were a spine I could wrap my hands around, from academics to pop fiction, Pulitzer Prize classics to *How to Get Your Child to Sleep Through the Night*. Books guided me to the best tours in Costa Rica and gave me hours of bedtime consorting with Gryffindors. And yet, bookshelf after bookshelf, I never found the one that would steer me out of the carpool pickup lane and back into my happy job on the hill.

Every time I turned my head, I'd see another capable ex-careerist brilliantly organizing travel for a soccer tournament, or having a ladies lunch or rushing home to a leaking dishwasher. Across America, so many valuable minds and ambitions were hanging back, leaning out, and fixing other people's boo-boos. *Hmmm*, I thought, maybe I could channel my bossy cheer and mix in some researched expertise to help these talented moms look out their window and see a more fulfilled snapshot of themselves.

So I started writing this book blindly. I plowed ahead, reading every self-help book and resource material about the current job market, and embarked on a chic recipe book for all women in search of a rewarding career.

All life's big changes are accomplished step-by-step. Every wedding planned, every baby born, every home built, every feast served, and every professional assignment involves consistent, incremental steps—bootstrapping your next career is no different.

That's where *Moms for Hire* comes to the rescue. Consider me your sisterly Princess Charming, riding in on a white horse (or a loaded minivan) to push and cheer you toward rewarding work.

You will have to do some lifting and follow directions, but lean on *Moms for Hire* to sherpa you through. *Moms for Hire* breaks down your climb into eight chapters that are stepping-stones to your new professional calling. These exercises are designed to be fun, informative, stimulating, and vital to your success.

Moms' reasons for going back to work vary widely. Some of you may need to earn a specific amount to sustain your family's livelihood. Others may want a more adult, mentally stimulating day; or you might crave your own identity and a paycheck you can claim as your own. You may be looking to reinvent your path completely, or maybe you're returning to a version of your previous career. Plenty of you are searching for a part-time opportunity, and some of you might happily discover that you're really satisfied exactly where you are. You might do a little digging and then discover that, for now, you are "good" staying home. This book will help you figure that out, too.

Reentry can feel impossible and traumatic. And the job of finding a new job can easily get lost in the business of mothering. A child with chicken pox, a new kitchen, a grandparent with a busted car, a wonky Wi-Fi system—all can easily fill a mom's day. When other people's needs grab your priority hours, years can go by without finding satisfying work. *Moms for Hire* will help you find the time and space to launch into the outside world.

My Bootstrapping Adventure

By many benchmarks, I had had a successful career. Then something shifted. Life moved forward, and I found myself looking out at new scenery. I was a fifty-plus-year-old mother of four who had hurdled and stumbled through the working world for over forty years. My first job was Pizza and Cotton Candy Chef at Nathan's Famous in the then-new Livingston, New Jersey, mall. Even as a teenager, I proudly loved the work, the camaraderie, and the paycheck.

Since then, I've worked at corporate jobs in Manhattan and at ad hoc kitchen-table spaces in Los Angeles, at corner offices in Hollywood and sketchy sets in far-off locations. I've navigated a career in a family business and rose to high-ranking positions in several entertainment industry jobs. I've quit and I've been fired. I've been overpaid and I've paid to be included in projects. Some freelance jobs have only lasted a few months, and one lasted thirteen years. I've been a boss and I've been bossed.

In my late twenties, I hit the jackpot and became a creative executive for Steven Spielberg's Amblin Entertainment. For thirteen years, I scouted, developed, and ultimately produced a few projects. My job description varied from project to project, but I was always in the mix. From *Goonies* to *Jurassic Park*; *Land Before Time* to *E.R*; *Indy Jones* to *Back to the Future*; *Little Rascals* to *Schindler's List*. It was a plum job, and I appreciated every moment.

Within those years, I married an aspiring producer and had three children. After each child, I recovered at home for a few weeks, found good childcare, then swung right back into the sixty-hour-a-week work zone. I never wanted to give up my satisfying job. My children were well cared for. My energy was plentiful. And even as I battled foot cancer, I kept working and parenting. I fiercely believed—and it was mostly true—that as long as I was happy, my family would be happy, too. Although I was too busy to remember it as such, for a good ten years my life would be described as *having it all*.

Ultimately, what drove me off the career ladder was a shattering family illness. My beloved, still youthful, brother was losing his battle to melanoma, and as things became dire, I realized I had to be with him during his last earthly months. I had always been a good girl worker bee, but suddenly my priorities took a seismic turn. When faced with real life-or-death suffering, I lost the taste for caring if someone else beat me to the next *Jurassic Park*. I downgraded my work efforts and, honestly, became a not-so-great employee. Obviously, I needed to recalibrate and find a new version of work that could keep me balanced.

I had never been this close to a death before, and as my brother's spirit passed, so did my interest in the movie business. A month after my brother died, I was let go from an already downsized job I could have done in my sleep.

The magnitude of losing a brother far outweighed my defeat of losing a job. So I went home to weep and figure out a next step. I kept myself plenty busy. One child was struggling with reading and turned out to have dyslexia, another wanted to give up the violin unless I listened more, and the third was always climbing the highest tree in the neighborhood and always in danger of falling without a net. It wasn't quite at crisis stage, but more child-rearing attention was required.

As my husband's business was thriving, it made the most sense for me to become a stay-at-home mother, and I began carrying the torch for my family's wellbeing. Quickly, we fell into the more traditional husband-wife division of labor. We were treated to a fourth "bonus" child, a daughter we named Billi after my departed brother, and we all became okay with this old-fashioned family status quo.

I knew I lived a fortunate lifestyle and never complained about my lost prestige and decreased disposable income; I was grateful to have healthy kids. Yet I was gradually spiraling into a low-grade funk, yearning for some previous version of myself. Looking to regain my inner Exec VP. But, I was stuck, held back by fears of the future and baffled about my next step.

When our children were ages three, twelve, seventeen, and eighteen, my husband suffered a massive heart attack and died on a movie set in Toronto. Our family's template changed forever. Overnight, I had to go back to work. I inherited my husband's movie production company, which had two films in postproduction and awaiting release, and several more in active development that, with a little pushing, could get made.

I had no option; I had to carry on for everyone. I was now in charge of everything: finances, the TV remote, car registration, college applications, and the various torrents of grief that would splash over us all daily. Holding it together became my job. I was powered by the instinctive drive to honor my husband's legacy, and a fierce resolve to not let my children be diminished or even defined by being fatherless. Instantly, I had to be the mom *and* the dad . . . and the sole breadwinner. There was no meandering, no ambivalence. I had to rush onto the closest on-ramp available, which was recalibrating a family production company.

Life went on. We moved homes. We got a puppy. The kids grew up, some went off to college, and we somehow thrived. My village of friends and family always helped, and we figured it out. However, seven years later, as I revisit my own mom-work path, I've discovered there is still no guidebook for women who are out there looking for that hidden on-ramp.

The average worker holds down twelve different jobs in a lifetime. Navigating professional off- and on-ramps is daunting for everyone. Being unemployed (or underemployed) can be lonely and demoralizing. In the current environment, educated women (51% of the college graduate population) are the first group to opt out of the workforce at a mean age of thirty-one years old, the same age that most people's career trajectories begin to soar. On average, moms opt out of employment for 2.7 years (Sylvia Ann Hewlett, 2010), and once these women come off the work ramp at this crucial career time frame, reentry is doubly difficult. And your equal pay potential drops exponentially.

And yet, sometimes as a mom, a daughter, a sister, you just have to go home. Sorry fellow feminists, but moms opting out isn't a weakness. At the time, it might have been the right decision. However, you discovered that the off-ramp was not a free ride. The scenic route had consequences, and today you might have your sights set on a different tomorrow.

It can be a paralyzing wait in that carpool lane. Every mom needs supportive, upbeat advice to vault the moat and outplay the gatekeeper. Let *Moms for Hire* be your sisterly portal to the castle of your choice.

Congratulations for taking that first step.

Time to go after your career mojo.

Note on Exercises: Reinstall Yourself with the Upgrade

Moms for Hire is divided into two parts.

In Part I, the first four steps are dedicated to repackaging yourself into an attractive and hire-able candidate. These steps will help organize your time and space; identify your connections and contacts; champion your transferable skills so you can effectively ask for a specific new career to hop back in. These starter steps One through Four are geared to college-educated woman who have been off the work wagon and now want back on.

Part II, Steps 5 to 8, will guide you through the nuts and bolts of your job hunt: résumés, cover letters, interviews, and other coaching tools. Spliced in with a continual vein of encouragement.

Throughout each of these eight steps are snapshot life stories of everyday moms and experts, interactive exercises and assignments. My hope is that you schedule one hour a day (sometimes a little more, sometimes a bit less) and commit to each of these incremental steps. As with any therapy or any diet, you might not see the results immediately. Believe in the increments. Although you might not yet see it, success is around the corner.

These exercises are then divided into two categories: *Reach-In* and *Reach-Out*. Both will stretch and strengthen your job hunting skills. Sometimes, you'll be asked to pick up a pen or click onto your computer and delve inward (*Reach-In Exercises*). Other workouts will prompt you off the couch, beyond your comfort zone, and towards other working folks (*Reach-Out Exercises*). Both will get you closer to where you want to be. Before you know it, you will have advanced with clarity and cheer.

PART I
BECOME AN ATTRACTIVE
JOB CANDIDATE

Step One

ACTIVATE YOUR
MOM FOR HIRE SWITCH

"You can, you should, and, if you are brave enough to start, you will."
—Stephen King, *On Writing: A Memoir of the Craft*

Congratulations! You're about to begin the bold journey of finding rewarding work. For any number of reasons, you stepped outside the working gates and are now ready to reenter. Let's start TODAY.

All transformational triumphs—losing weight, finding a mate, learning a language, becoming sober, buying a home, bringing home a child—are achieved in incremental, daily steps. *Moms for Hire* has divided the steps of ramping back into the workforce into hour-long segments so you can make real change and actualize your goals without having to put your life on hold. For some, these segments might take less than sixty minutes. Great! Others might really get into the exercise and keep at it for longer. Also great! As with any task, your focus and motivation can vary. Just stick with it and keep at the process of getting hired. Dig in, stay honest, and follow the course.

All of us think about how our lives might have taken other paths and that's okay to speak those secrets, and maybe even necessary. Within these pages, I encourage you to express your job fantasies and job regrets. These exercises will help you use both to find your own true calling.

For me, a single mother of four essentially thriving kids, my little secret is: *Sure, I absolutely love being a mother. I am grateful. And I feel that motherhood is an amazing accomplishment. Still, for me, being a mom isn't enough, and I want more!*

There is always a road not yet taken. Today's the day to explore inward and bravely fantasize about what a "win" might look like.

Your desire to reboot a work plan may start with an ache for a professional compliment, or a dream of a shingle with your name on it. Maybe you keep catching yourself staring with envy at another mom's Prada work shoes, or you have an absolute conviction that your investment ideas are better than your husband's. It could be an empty moment on a Tuesday morning after drop-off when you realize all you have to do until pick-up is make the beds and fight the crab grass, or that liberating realization that your teenager doesn't need you anymore to drive him to the mall or check his homework. Or all of it. You are ready.

Maybe you know that your household would be better off with a second paycheck, or one is sorely needed. Perhaps you remember that you once had a professional life and know you have more to contribute outside of what you do for your family. Certainly, the scenic route has given you some gratifying perks and probably your off-ramped time was family-necessary, but you may be feeling that parenting is not the only thing you want or need to do. In any event, it's time to plan for a career reentry when your kids are launched, or even long before then.

Pick a Single Hour Every Day: the job of finding a job

Consider today to be the first day of a new job—the job of finding a job. Commit to one hour per day, five days a week, of inviting these exercises into your life. Commit to yourself as you would commit to a boss. Commit to yourself as you would expect an employee to commit to you, if you were the boss. The trick is to commit. Turn off your phone. Don't you dare fold another laundered t-shirt. Ban social texting and emailing. Shut out your busy world and distractions, and focus on your transformation.

It's only an hour a day, but for those who have been away from the punch-clock and a boss, scheduling this single hour daily can be challenging. Set your alarm clock for one hour earlier, switch from homemade marinara sauce to Prego, or give away a few carpool runs. Find and protect that single hour in every workday and commit to changing your life. Consistency is key to forming any new habit; protect your sacred *Mom for Hire* hour as you launch into the eight steps of this book. Once you have strictly calendared your daily hour, grab a pen, write the date at the top of the page, and you're off!

This step will help suss out how you spend your day when the kids are in school. You'll take a look at your fears and see that they may not be so bad after all. Determine where your strengths lie and declare your Next Chapter status to family and friends.

Hour Goals

Hour One:	**Claim** your daily hour and log your time.
Hour Two:	**Reveal** your fears.
Hour Three:	**Evaluate** your "launch-ability."
Hour Four:	**Visualize** your ideal job.
Hour Five:	**Reveal** your transferrable skills and announce your job hunt.

"*Think Outside the Mom.*"
—Jamie Cole

Keep a Quick Time Log: every day for five days

When you are not punching an office time clock, your unmonitored hours can somehow float away. Let's calculate how you spend your day, hour by hour. It's important to track what you do every hour so you can see if time is working for you. Scheduling and budgeting your time is a much harder task when you're not expected to be at an office for a consistent and particular time.

On the following page, you'll find a handy Log Sheet that breaks the week into days and hours. Starting today and every day this week, pay attention to how your hours elapse. If you've ever joined Weight Watchers, you know they suggest accounting for every calorie so you can gauge what and when you ate. If you are (or were) a lawyer or accountant, you logged your billable hours in 15-minute increments. So pay attention to your time for this first week, preferably as the day progresses, but at least before you go to bed. It will prove immensely valuable, and it only takes a total of five minutes. Soon, this log will become an essential tool as you scan through your calendar for *empty* or *extra* workable hours that you could use toward your next chapter.

Hour Log, week of: _____

	Mon.	Tues.	Weds.	Thurs.	Fri.
6am					
7am					
8am					
9am					
10am					
11am					
noon					
1pm					
2pm					
3pm					
4pm					
5pm					
6pm					
7pm					
8pm					
9pm					
10pm					
11pm					

■ Home   ■ Kids/Family   ■ Fitness & Beauty   ■ Volunteer/Training/Spec   ■ Compensated Work   ■ Free Time

Extra Hour Log pages available for download on DeborahJelinNewmyer.com. Follow the *MomForHire* link to Bonus Take Aways/Worksheets.

Hour One
Time, Time, Time.

"Where did my day go?" Let's measure the baseline of your most ordinary Mom Day. When you are the sergeant for other people's busy schedules, there may be no such thing as a regular day. Yet, if you want to swing back into the working world, you have to uncover and compensate for your own time, too. Let's start with a look at your day-in-the-life with this first *Reach-In* exercise.

It's time to get granular about time. Have a look at your weekday schedule in terms of buckets: morning hours, school hours, afterschool hours, and evenings. It's time to figure out what you are really doing with your time, so complete the exercise on the next page to get an idea of what your buckets of daily time look like.

As Caretaker-to-Many, Don't Forget to Caretake Yourself
Even if you are not bringing home a paycheck, you are entitled to pleasure. You cannot be a caregiver to everyone else. How do you budget "Mom Regenerating Time" into your family schedule? If you have forgotten, here's what your "ME" time could look like:

❑ Exercising
❑ Gardening
❑ Reading
❑ Watching television
❑ Social media and games
❑ Socializing in person with friends
❑ Looking for a snazzy new job
❑ Learning a new language
❑ Taking classes
❑ Massage, manicure
❑ Spirituality/Religion
❑ Other (ame it)

Reach-In Exercise

Complete this exercise to get an idea of what your buckets of daily time look like.

<u>Mornings:</u>

I wake up at _____.

My children and mate wake up at _____.

I prepare the household's breakfast and lunches _____ times a week.

I drive the kids to school _____ times a week. Drop-off time _____.

I volunteer on school committees _____ hours a week.

<u>During School Hours (9 a.m.–3 p.m.):</u>

I am not alone _____ hours a day (other parents, my parents, spouse/partner, friends).

I am alone _____ hours a day; either busy with home upkeep or working on a personal project.

<u>After School:</u>

I pick up my kids from school at _____ p.m., _____ times a week.

I drive my children to afternoon sports or art or dance classes _____ times a week.

I have kids with extra needs (academic, physical, or emotional) _____ hours _____ a week.

I volunteer for my church/temple/charity/organization/friend _____ hours a week.

<u>Evenings:</u>

I cook dinner _____ times a week.

I help my children with their homework and other evening rituals _____ times a week.

I have out-of-home meetings or classes _____ evenings a week.

I have out-of-home weekend classes or responsibilities _____ hours a week.

I keep up with regular exercise and recreational activities _____ times a week for _____ hours.

I go to the market or run other household errands (including bill paying) _____ hours a day.

I have extra childcare help _____ times a week for _____ hours a day.

My spouse is an active parent and shares _____ percent of the home and family upkeep.

*"You have to put on your own oxygen mask before you put on others'.
It's a good metaphor for parenting."*
—Amanda Peet, actress

Classic Mom Botch

Make sure you are not always at the bottom of the family pyramid. You need to find a way to treat yourself well too.   If you are the only one sacrificing for the family's greater good, you will end up making everyone unhappy. Too often, your sustaining joys get pushed off until tomorrow or next week or next season. Schedule "ME" time to take care of Mom's personal needs. Do not wait until everyone is perfectly satiated before you do. You are not being bratty by taking care of yourself. If you stretch yourself too thin or if you become doormatted by your stay-at-home status, you do no one any good.

Please begin scheduling and marking off official time for you. Whatever quest you choose—professional, artistic, social—you cannot be passive about it. Take ownership of your future, and budget in an organized (even sacred) time for refreshing yourself. One hour at a time.

DEB TELLS ALL

At a few junctures while writing *Moms for Hire*, I considered naming the book *The Bossy Girlfriend's Guide to Career Success*. To me, being **bossy** is one of my most transferable skills, and without the support of my many bossy girlfriends, I would be a sorry puddle. Lately, the word "bossy" has taken on the meaning of a politically incorrect, offensive-to-some slur. Sure, I could switch up the semantics and safely call myself *assertive* or *confident* or *sassy*. But that's no fun: I really am bossy. I am also kind, caring, and honest. And I believe that my opinions can be valuable. So I stand loud and firm on my bossy terrain. My apologies if the word is currently out of favor; it happens to happily fit me. I believe we all need *a bossy girl-friend* in our lives. Find yours. I am here to be that upbeat, surprisingly unjudgmental, yet still authoritative voice sitting on your shoulder and pushing you along.

I also found that I had tireless curiosity and compassion for how people "lead their lives." I loved hearing the answer to: How did you get to live your life in a ski-town? Why did you have so many children? How did you become a movie titan? Why are your song lyrics always so sad? Where does your artistic drive come from? Where'd you buy all those great shoes? I found myself especially interested in how other mothers navigated their life path. The double identity of being both a mom and a careerist never ceases to engage me. There are so many tangents we all travel—from coloring-within-the lines to gravestone shopping. I like it all. And am constantly inquiring ***How Did YOU Do It?*** Granted many folks start out with either genetic advantages or unfair obstacles. Plenty of choices and circumstances are made for us, and our fiber can gel at a very early age. But it's once our free will clicks in that most intrigues me . . . and I love musing with any fellow grown-up as to how they settled into their adult persona. How did they face adversity? How do they manage their lives? How did their families' values imprint upon them? How does their socio- and psychohistory effect their productivity, their everyday routines? And their happiness?

Throughout years of job interviews, dates, and bonding with real friends, my conversations always swing around to "how did we turn out this way?" My arsenal of sociological curiosity and that eternal bossiness lead me to constantly ask every woman about their life path. From those scores and scores of conversations—some formal, some intimate—I put together the snapshots of these women's work/play lives. These ***How Did SHE Do It*** boxes are part testimonials/part case studies/part my vivid remembrances of our conversations . . . a.k.a. *LIFE SLICES*. In most cases, I got the gist of their story told through my lenses. I cannot thank these women enough for opening up a slice of their lives for others to read. Here is one to start:

How Did SHE Do It?
She felt stuck. She admitted she wanted MORE. She periscoped.

Jennifer S., A+ mother of two, former ER nurse, professional organizer

Jennifer always had a lot of bounce. Everyone she met would immediately register Jen as a funny, confident, and stellar stay-at-home mom. Her son (eight) is a gifted first baseman, and her daughter (twelve) loves the trapeze and can really converse in French. Her kids get along well with each other, and they laugh at her jokes. Last April, she ran a school book fair and raised $17,000; it would not have happened without Jennifer's persistence and organizational prowess.

She was deservedly proud of her parenting routines: every Saturday morning, her husband and son hand-wash both cars, and every Sunday the family chats with the waffle guy at the local farmer's market. She hosts a weekly dinner for her parents and siblings in her stunningly remodeled family kitchen. Pretty idyllic. Jen's got a ladder in every upstairs bedroom and an earthquake kit in every car. She is a founding member of

Continued . . .

---

a book & social media awareness club that recently began concentrating on YA books so that all the moms know what lies ahead for their teen readers. She is intimidatingly prepared and considered "nicely bossy." She was a registered nurse until she had her first child and still arranges every item in her fridge, pantry, and washroom by "date purchased."

Yet, for all her uber-Mom scheduling, Jen began to feel personally undirected. While all of her household lists and back-up plans were in perfect order, she hadn't found the time to get her hair dyed in six months. She could not shake the feeling that "a parade was passing her by," so she periscoped her options. She hit upon her "aha" moment when she was asked to help clean out her recently deceased 94-year-old grandpa's house. Getting deep into the trenches of someone else's stuff highlighted Jen's untapped, savant-like skill set: putting things "In Their Place." Jen also knew she had to be her own boss and be in charge of her own schedule. She surfed online and found a supportive job group—the National Association of Professional Organizers—and she joined up.

Now, she could put a name to her next career: Professional Organizer. Lickity-split, she had business cards made up, and she was launched. In the beginning, Jen volunteered her systemizing skills to friends with needy closets, basements, and libraries but quickly became compensated for a job she loves and that validates her new-found expertise. Once Jennifer boldly admitted that she wanted more, she had the tools, the talent, and the networking connections to figure out how to get it. You're next.

"So the pie isn't perfect? Cut it into wedges. Stay in control, and never panic."
–Martha Stewart

Daily Do List

❏ Scheduled one hour a day to commit to *Moms for Hire.*

❏ Took stock of how I spent my hours on an ordinary day.

❏ Spent five minutes today logging my Daily Schedule.

Hour Two
Uncloak Your F*#%in' Fears

Now that you've begun the habit of daily *Mom for Hire* time, it's important to take a little time (or the next hour) to see what might be stopping you from forging ahead. What's really going on when the clock reads noon and you are still stuck in your sweats and slippers? What's stopping you from figuring out how to get back inside the workday fortress?

Fear is one of our most natural instincts. All living creatures have fear in their arsenal of reflexes. It can protect. It can empower. It can paralyze. Sometimes fear can stream through your body like adrenaline, enabling you to lift a car off your son or ski down a double black chute. And other times fear will make you stutter during a presentation or sleep with all the lights on.

With your children under your care, your worry factor rises exponentially. Will they get hurt? Will they hurt others? Will they be happy? Will they make others happy? Will they be productive? It seems to never end. The fear door is never closed when it comes to your kids. And for most moms, your maternal fears can supersede your own worries.

And then, just when you have your kids somewhat settled, your personal anxieties can spring forth. Will an earthquake hit my home? A tornado? Will my husband have an affair? Will I get an invitation to the next in-crowd party?

Today, let's shine a spotlight on your fears. What is stopping you from hurtling into your next chapter? What the f*#k are you afraid of? Tell all. The only way to progress past an obstacle is to recognize the block, state it, face it, and then vault it. You are not alone in being stymied by uncertainty, by free-floating anxiety.

So many famous actresses are afraid of public speaking . . .

So many professional golfers break into a sweat before each big tee shot. . .

So many great students fight back choking before exams . . .

Reach-In Exercise: BE FEARLESS WITH YOUR FEAR LIST.

What concrete obstacle is holding you back? What scenario haunts you when you imagine going back to work? Is it exciting? Terrifying? Both?

My Examples:

- *If I don't vacuum the carpet every day, my son might have another asthma attack.*
- *If my daughter loses her competition music and cannot practice, I will have to cancel a meeting and run to purchase a new copy.*
- *If my job runs late one day, and my sitter is out sick, my kid will be sitting alone at school, and I'll feel like a terrible mother.*

Now, Brave One, let's list what you most fear about going back to work:

What is *really* stopping you?

If I go back to work, my family will:

_____

_____

_____

If I go back to work, can I succeed in the ever-changing work world?

_____

_____

_____

If I don't go back to work . . . what will be next for me? For my family?

_____

_____

_____

Most of these fears are versions of universal mom dread that you may not be "good enough" as a parent, a spouse, or a worker. Guilt hangs around every mom's neck and threatens to choke back her career. Your mixed feelings are valid and need to be spoken and written down without judgment. Your fears need to be illuminated, then bleached away. Once you identify the specific fear holding you back, you will have a better chance of finding a job that can match your absolute skills and desires.

Hypothetical Scenario Fest: With many of my primal life decisions (which house to live in, where the kids should go to school, how to spend my money, etc.), my process for defusing my anxiety of any impending scenario is to name that haunting fear and then carry it through to its every possible conclusion. I go through my list . . . and it calms me through:

> *"What's the worst that could happen?"*
> *"What's the best-case scenario?"*
> *"It's been working out so far—why would that change now?"*
> *"Even if the worst happens, is there a silver kernel to be derived?"*

Reach-In Exercise: NOW PIGEONHOLE YOUR FEAR INVENTORY.

We all have sleepless nights. But the more precisely you can define your fear, the sooner you can strategically find a solution. And move onward.

Listing your fears is the first step to banishing them. Often, when you picture a specific fear, you discover the fear to be a bogeyman, lurking in dark corners; and once exposed, that fear cannot survive the light. Next, look at your fear list, become strategic with each item, and look for a practical solution. We know that it never works to be an ostrich with your fears. If you try to hide them or let them float around unexamined, they always win.

For example, you might think you won't have time to spend with your kids if you go back to work. It's way too soon to license that fear and allow it to stop you from looking for a job. Maybe you could negotiate flex-time with a potential employer as part of your compensation package. Maybe your kids would even prefer to participate in an after-school program instead of getting picked up at 3 p.m. Or maybe you should only be looking for part-time work. The bottom line is that naming and talking through the fear will ease your anxiety and get you on track to be brave.

Now that you have listed your biggest worries, your deepest anxieties . . . how do you move past them? Some fears can be reasoned away or solved with a practical or creative solution. Often, you can look at fear and call it "irrational" and dismiss it. Other fears are more stubborn . . . and you actually have to live with them as you would an annoying neighbor.

There are methods for dealing with lingering fears. Some overcome anxiety through relaxation methods, or reorganize their life to be less stressful, or drink less caffeine or make the leap to prescribed medical adjustments (no judgment, they work too). Some find calmness in talking things out with a friend or a professional.

Most often, banishing your (real or imagined) fears requires a lot of willpower, and a conscious effort to convert your fear into positive adrenaline. There are always stories of the camera-shy journalist who hates audiences. Or the brilliant law scholar who must stand on her head to calm before every test. Or the assistant who needs to recruit someone else to ask her boss for a raise. Once you've listed your fears, you've got to consciously decide that you want to outsmart them. There are plenty of tricks for the stutterer, the clutcher, the publicity-shy. And if logic or relaxation techniques or outside support don't heal all your worries, you'll have to adjust to that disability as you would to any handicap: compartmentalize it . . . and carry forward with the goods you've got.

Cherish Your Core Four (or Two or Five or Twelve) Friends
When You Are Feeling the Fear . . . Girlfriends Are a Girl's Best Friend.

Friends come in all shapes and sizes, and we have different call-outs for different friends. One friend might be a perfect sidekick at a dance party but would show no interest in your crush on MSNBC's Chris Matthews. You might depend on another friend for the soccer game scheduling or finding the best movie for Saturday night, but you would never reveal your darkest truths to her. Some friends don't mind if you only call them when you need something, and others get insulted if you don't return a text within two hours. You might see some acquaintances nearly every day, and some intimate friends you might only connect with yearly. Then there are your Core Four friends. The friends you might compete with but who always have your back. The friends who don't mind you calling at 5 a.m. Who you never have to ask to be invited over, or apologize for missing an event. They know you love them, and you trust them always to be honest and still love you.

They are your "in case of emergencies" friends. Other than your immediate family, they are your first responders. They are on your speed dial:

- When your car breaks down miles away from home.
- When your son wins the football sectionals.
- When you need someone to sit with you through chemo treatment.
- When your daughter didn't get into the college she was hoping for.

My good friend Marianne found her Core Four at regularly scheduled tennis lessons. She competed with them twice a week. All four were mothers; none of them were public school teachers or single parents like she was . . . but they were all active in her life. She could ask them anything, and they would have a helpful opinion. When she was ready to switch careers . . . maybe to retire . . . maybe to go back to school . . . maybe to move to another district. They all helped her. They vision-mapped with her. They took and re-took her Talent/Expert Test. And they were her sounding board, network advisors, and general pushy girlfriends as she launched herself into her next professional chapter.

Find your Core Friends. You can have only one or three or ten, but check in with them often. Your Core Four could be local, or only a Facetime away. Either way, become their generous but honest backboard in return.

Daily Do List

❑ Listed my fears. Professional? Domestic? Self-Esteem?

❑ Analyzed my listed fears and outsmarted some with practical solves.

❑ Knighted and treasured my Core Four Friends.

❑ Marched alongside my more permanent fears and lived with them.

❑ Spent five minutes tracking my hours into the Weekly Log.

Hour Three
Evaluate Your Launch-Readiness

Only you can determine your "launch-ability" and readiness to return to the workforce, whether you have to, want to, or a combination of both. Personally, I am a multitasker and at my happiest when I'm working hard and have a lot of juggling going on. I get more accomplished when I'm firing on a lot of cylinders. Sweating always makes me bolder and more flexible. These work cravings might change as I march onward through life. For me and for now, a little stress acts as a positive motivator.

By now, you are enough of a grown-up to know what makes you tick. If this seems like a skipable step, think again! The best way to land a job is to be *ready* to land a job. Your fear inventory gleaned a lot of information about your hesitation. Now you need to do your homework about what kind of employee you are. What helps your best qualities emerge? What are your challenging traits?

Let's be real. It's a complicated world filled with obstacles that can thwart you from that dream job. Some barriers fall within your *Mom for Hire* control, and some do not. The employing world is not always fair. Discrimination is not in your imagination. Although there are laws against it, there's no doubt that ethnic background, disabilities, motherhood, financial debt, sexual orientation, etc., can undermine you getting hired.

Current statistics don't lie. Professional profiling and prejudgments are real. Hiring and salary disparities for women and ethnic groups cannot be sugarcoated. However, don't let that stop you from trying. Do not allow the unchangeable factors of your skin color, religion, or gender deter you from pushing forward. You deserve to get a job that makes you happy. And even though the odds are not always in your favor, and you might lose out on some jobs with that typical employer (we know who he is . . .), there is still plenty you can control. Fair employment is a birthright. *Moms for Hire* will be on your side rooting for you to bootstrap yourself into rewarding opportunities.

You are an exponentially more attractive candidate once you've rid yourself of job-seeking ambivalence. I want to encourage you to be brave and indulge in this *reaching in* step. Work it!

Fair Warning: Get ready . . . Becoming a *Mom for Hire* means you will need to adjust and maybe surrender a few specific pieces of your current lifestyle. This may actually be exciting for you, but if this thought sends you off on a nail-biting vortex of worry, that's okay, too. What is most important at this juncture is being honest with yourself. Let's frankly think through all the following questions and assess your real readiness.

How Did SHE Do It?
She looked inside and liked what she saw.
Jocelyn S., mother of two, ex-public defender, yoga instructor

When Jocelyn was in fifth grade, she wanted to be President of the United States. She was smart. She could sing. She was the whole ball of wax. She was privileged enough to go to great schools and was determined to turn all that privilege into a stimulating life. At her Ivy League college back East, Jocelyn met her husband. They moved to California, and after a few bumps in her twenties, Jocelyn became a very happy public defender in Orange County, California.

For five years, Jocelyn drove an hour to work and loved being in her professional zone. She defended plenty of decent folks who needed her support and was extremely comfortable advocating for others in front of a stern judge and a packed courtroom. Jocelyn had found her calling.

And then she had a baby girl. She took a maternity leave, and a seismic switch turned: Jocelyn could not go back to that world she loved. She admitted with huge regrets that she would probably never get to defend a death penalty case . . . and so, she decided to figure out a career alternative. She tried work for the ACLU. Also, she had another child and surprised herself at how much pleasure she got from her awesome daughters. And then how much she loved taking summers off to spend with the family. Whenever she sank into feeling unaccomplished, she'd take a long run or a challenging yoga class.

After nearly ten years away from active lawyering, Jocelyn took a hard look at what made her happiest. She discovered *her dream picture frame* (see page 140) was doing a handstand on a paddleboard in the middle of a stormy lake. And she enrolled in a 400-hour yoga training class.

At first she rolled up her carpets and taught in her living room. Cut to today, and Jocelyn is one of the most beloved yoga teachers in LA. Local yogis flock to her classes and retreats. She discovered that she never lost her lawyerly skills. She is still in front of a jury of people and persuades them to dig deep, challenge themselves, and find a peaceful truth.

"How can I get fired from this job?"
—Nicole Wyler, ex-high school vice principal and gym mom to Jr. Olympic gymnast

Reach-In Exercise: HOW IMPORTANT IS WORKING (OUTSIDE YOUR HOME) TO YOU?

Has your family's situation changed recently and you need to find a job immediately to financially support your family and lifestyle?

- Is your Next Chapter calling a more flexible desire of "It would be nice if I could find a job that fits into my mothering schedule"?
- Do you have the financial luxury of looking around for a while to find your fantasy job?
- Can you financially and schedule-wise afford going back to school to recareer?
- Can you afford an investment in a future project or afford the lag time for a start-up to succeed?

If you've answered YES to at least two of these questions and—somehow—you know you're ready to leap into the workforce, still it might not be for tomorrow. You might first need to:

- Wait until your youngest goes to kindergarten in September.
- Help your mother through her kidney transplant recovery for two months.
- Send your oldest off to college (but don't wait until send your youngest).

Even if you cannot begin working immediately, start in with the *Moms for Hire* quest anyway. Eventually, the on-ramp fever will take over, and it's good to start strategizing and figuring out your desires and skills as soon as possible.

After you've determined to forge ahead as a *Mom for Hire*, then you should also begin to:

- Look out for affordable and comfortable childcare.
- Arrange help from family or friends to pick up the kids from school.
- Accept that going back to work means you won't be as much fun on weeknights.
- Get used to being okay with your kids' lunches not always being perfect (leftover pasta is character building!).

Continued . . .

- Admit you might not be able to watch TV for more than a few minutes at a time.
- Understand you might be exhausted after work and the family's usual Monday night trip to the ice cream parlor will have to wait until the weekend.
- Be prepared to handle more whining when, on Saturday, the kids have to go with you to the grocery store, dry cleaners and car wash.
- Instead of spending the month shopping, decorating, and hosting for the Holidays, re-up your Amazon Prime account and squeeze it all into a few rushed December days.
- Push your own career potential to the top of the family's pyramid.
- Switch your Tuesday noon tennis foursome and schedule a time for Dad to be in charge of the Sunday breakfast adventure.
- Resist the urge to always lend a helping hand. Set a limit on your volunteering impulses.

When you announce your intention to return to work, expect some family kickback. The scenery will change for the whole family, and you might not get full support from the jostled homefront. Converting your *domestic hours* into *working hours* will be an adjustment for everyone. Sorry for them, but you have paid your caretaking dues, and now it's time to reshuffle and to share the domestic homework with your perfectly capable home team.

Your Finance Nitty Gritty

Are all these changes worth the additional income? Think about this a bit. If you loved your prekid job, but the money you will earn going back into your chosen field will barely cover the expense of driving three kids to three separate after school activities . . . Good to know. But still, even if the finances reaped do not amount to a tremendous net gain—they will eventually. Plus, being stimulated by a career has real power beyond the monetary. Even if your paycheck is minimal, it will be yours. Do not ever let anyone shame you into believing your career return will be "worthless." Professional satisfaction will have a tangible effect on your happiness, your daughter's empowerment and your son's view of women in the world.

We will get to finances in Step Four, but for now, start channeling your inner grown-up regarding financial questions. What is the value of the additional income you may be collecting? What's the cost of your departure into the marketplace? In Step Four, we will guide you through a calculation of your household costs. For now, start gathering your fixed bills (mortgage, insurance, tuition, etc.), variable credit cards, and bank receipts together into one big bowl. Financial literacy is never taught enough in school, and too often talking about money and negotiating is not considered polite conversation. Wrong. In fact, financial intelligence is extremely empowering. We all need more financial know-how and more guts to speak about how family money is earned, spent, and saved.

Hopefully, these questions have prompted you to definitively assess if you are ready to "on-ramp." Ambivalence is obvious and a buzzkill to any employer, so answer these questions honestly now. Even if you see things you'd rather not see, better to know now and start changing.

How Did SHE Do It?
She became unstuck.

Charlotte B., former TV executive and producer, single mother of two

Right out of college, Charlotte got a job as an entry-level assistant in a Postproduction company. She was a fast-and-smart learner, and in time, she rose up the ranks from a TV editor to a TV executive to a TV producer. Her rewarding TV jobs carried her through raising two sons and giving a divorce. After a few dry years of coasting, these jobs became less energizing, and she found herself in a position outside the television industry that had sustained her for two decades. Charlotte was bewildered as to how to regain professional joy and how to pay her bills.

She wandered a bit, her boys grew more independent, and she decided to go back to school and got a master's degree in Spiritual Psychology to become a certified Life Coach. She discovered she loved guiding others in their life course struggles, and she quickly launched a successful practice with dozens of clients. Ironically, it turned out that becoming a life coach for clients brought her full circle back to her own career. In the hours she spent working with clients, she simultaneously did the Life work on herself. She analyzed what would be her ideal job, and revealed—with confidence—her dormant talents, her transferable skills, and her future cravings.

When she put out feelers to her past contacts and talent, all those years of hard, smart work and loyalty were returned to her. She was offered a position with someone she hadn't worked with in years. Sure, she was older, but she knew her stuff and she still had allies. Charlotte took the job for a newer network; first as a consultant, then as a supervising executive, and now as a producer. Oh, and she still life-coaches a handful of clients regularly.

Charlotte had to reach inside and figure out how she wanted to reinvent herself. And it turned out that after she did the searching, she was refreshed and rejiggered, and became a stellar candidate for the job she was most qualified to do.

"Dream your own dream or you will end up being hired onto someone else's dream."
—Elizabeth English, headmaster, Archer School for Girls

<u>**Daily Do List**</u>

❑ Coat-checked my ambivalence.

❑ Gave birth to some new courage.

❑ Challenged my fears to leave me alone.

❑ Kept tally of my time.

Hour Four
Visualize Your Ideal Job

Today, let's have some fun! Time to fantasize about your future!

During this hour, dismiss all your worries of not being good enough. Ignore any fears of letting down your children or spouse. Table any anxiety over possible failure. Override the numbness of ambivalence. Push yourself to enjoy some fantasies!

Fantasizing about your own future is not always easy. Even in 2017, many of us have betrayed Sheryl Sandberg and slid into a traditional caregiving role, becoming the family's "responsible one." Maybe you've compromised your dreams and pressed pause on your ambitions. Thus, even daydreaming about yourself takes a backseat. Instead of pushing your career, you've dedicated 10,000 hours to becoming an expert at reminding little ones to say "thank you," brush their teeth, not beat up their brother, make that goal, aim for the A+, and—of course—always be kind. You've deflected the accolades, maybe gotten a mom haircut, and taken on a rounder shape.

Let's spend today advocating for yourself. Just you. You've earned the right to spend a few hours focusing on your best professional options. Let's start by recalling your first response to "What do you want to be when you grow up?" and remember whatever high school "most likely to . . . " moniker you were given, and your favorite college clubs. Then, allow yourself some inappropriate career wishes. Explore your forbidden joys. Escape your parental cover and go shopping for your fantasy job. If you are having fun with this career role-playing, this "hour" might absorb you for more than an hour, and that's okay. Yahoo—dream your dream job!

<u>Find Your "If Only I . . . "</u>

Surely some of your friends already have a dream job:

- One friend talks nonstop about a backyard beekeeper business, and she thinks, "If only I . . ."
- Your sorority sister dreams of running for mayor in her hometown. "If only I . . ."
- A part-time lawyer seems determined to switch careers to be a helicopter pilot. "If only I . . ."
- My accountant has a great idea for a television show. "If only I . . ."
- I have always, always wanted to be the location scout for The Amazing Race, "If only I . . ."

"Success is not final, failure is not fatal. It is the courage to continue that counts."
—Winston Churchill

If you don't yet have a specific job-craving, let's generate one now! The following exercise will get you to express and decode a fantasy job (or a few). *Moms for Hire* cannot promise you will 100 percent nab that perfect dream job, but dream anyway! It'll help you focus and allow your life to get bigger, wider, and deeper. Think big. Once you can uncover and verbalize your ideal job, then you will have a goal, and it will be easier to home in on a job that fits multiple criteria (if not all) of your dream job. *Dream* first . . . then *do*.

Vision Mapping Romp

If you're already a Pinterest person, you've started to play with vision mapping and are cyber-collecting images that make you happy. Last year, as a thank you gift from her boss, my eldest daughter Sofi was given a retreat weekend at a spa, and kindly, she invited me along. We hiked and soaked. We greeted the sunset on a ropes course, and in an odd twist, we rode a mechanical bull. One free hour, we were scheduled into a "vision mapping seminar." Reluctantly, we wandered into a room of magazines and poster boards. We put aside our lame discomfort and jumped into this vision mapping exercise. Throughout the years I have quested after any source of personal revelations, be it therapeutic, psychic, yogic, or even the random Buzzfeed quiz. I enjoy digging for what might make me happier and more effective in the world. Surpisingly, this old-school version of Pinterest was a blast and pleasantly revealing. Give it a go.

Reach-In Exercise: YOUR DO-IT-YOURSELF VISION MAPPING WHIRL.

- First, visit your corner magazine kiosk (or dig into your recycling bin) and pick out at least four magazines. Vary your selection: a fashion magazine, business periodical, sport or gossip rag, foodie magazine, or any of the reams of catalogs that arrive on your doorstep—whatever seems energetic and entertaining (*Vanity Fair, Dwell,* the *Week, Martha Stewart, Armstrong Garden Center, Us Weekly,* etc.).
- Sit down and flip through all these (hopefully, recyclable) pages. With joyful abandon, rip out the images, letters, phrases, and quotes that immediately speak to you. Do not edit this tear-and-gather quest; just go for it.
- Now, get in touch with your crafty side. Borrow a glue stick from your fourth grader's backpack and mount the images on a poster board. You will be stunned by the assortment of attractions it reveals.

Perhaps every sweater and teapot you chose was decorated with flowers—puzzling, since you already have three teapots and a closet full of cashmeres—but the flower motif is undeniable. Clearly, that not-so-hidden craving to open a flower shop or start an urban gardening business just got uncovered. If this is the case, you might want to find the closest flower market and offer to design the flowers for your friend's next birthday party. Offer that as her present, and—*voilà!*—you'll start launching your new business.

Or maybe you always planned to go back to law school, and that degree seemed to be the dangling, unfinished annoyance of your career. Whenever you had a free parcel of time, you intended to start studying to take the LSAT. And yet during this vision mapping romp, every picture you impulsively chose was of animals or people tending animals. Maybe there is a reason you rescued two dogs, three cats, and a parrot last year. Think about volunteering for an animal clinic or combine those skills and call to see if your local vet might need some paralegal help.

Not every vision map is so obviously revealing, but it's worth an hour to jumpstart the excitement of heading back into your career.

Reach-Out Version: THROW A VISION MAPPING PARTY.

A great way to publicly expand on your *Moms for Hire* quest is to have a vision mapping party. Supportive peers can make job hunting much easier, and honestly, the more mags the better. Add a social hour onto your book club, your weekly hike, or your PTA event! Next time your friends gather, ask each to bring four magazines or catalogues and go on a vision fest.

Next, grab a pen and sit down with the passion list below. Again, without second-guessing, boldly circle any category that speaks to you or sparks your interest.

What do you talk about at cocktail parties? What section of the newspaper do you flip to first? Take out your phone—what are your go-to apps? Don't hold back. Knee-jerk your responses. Don't be afraid to admit your oddest job craving. And if a hidden passion isn't on this list, feel free to add it now.

Your Passion List:

Now it's your turn to pick your passion. Circle the topics that interest you the most. What do you love? What's the first thought that comes to mind in the morning? What do you talk about most with your peers?

- Adventure Recreation
- Advertising/Publicity
- Aging & Ailments
- Animals
- Apps & Blogging
- Architecture
- Art
- Artificial Intelligence
- Aviation
- Bargains & Deals
- Books or Magazines
- Bosses & Coworkers
- Bugs & Bees
- Building Things
- Cars & Bikes
- Childcare
- College
- Community Service
- Computer Games
- Computer Software
- Consumer Advocacy
- Cooking
- Counseling
- Corporate Branding
- Creating Beauty
- Energy
- Environmental Issues
- Family
- Fashion
- Fertility & Birth Control

- Film
- Fitness
- Flight & Space
- Food & Diet
- Foreign Languages
- Games
- Garden & Bugs
- Genetics & Biotech
- Healthcare Advocacy
- History
- Human Resources
- Human Rights
- International Affairs
- Investments
- Jewelry Design
- Job Desires
- Journalism
- Landscaping
- Law
- Machines & Engineering
- Management
- Math
- Money
- Music & Radio
- Offshoring/Mining
- Personality Quirks
- Philosophy
- Photography
- Politics
- Public Policy

- Public Speaking
- Retail
- Real Estate
- Religion & Spirituality
- Research
- Retail & Shopping
- Robotics
- Salary
- Sales & Marketing
- Science
- School/Education
- Sex & Dating
- Sports
- Social Media & Apps
- Substance Abuse
- Taxes & Accounting
- Teaching
- Technology
- Telecommunications
- Television
- Terrorism
- Theater
- Therapy
- Travel
- Urban Planning
- Web Design
- Weekend Plans
- Writing
- Your Gadgets

After forty years of various jobs and twenty-five years of raising four children, lately as a single mom, I crave a job where I don't have to be *the initiator*. For decades, I was the one who arrived earliest and brewed the first pot of coffee, but also turned off the lights and locked up at night. And for the last ten years, I have been the person to invent and run whatever project I was involved in. So for my next job, I would like to throw the keys to someone and let them drive. I know this would mean giving up a degree of control and days off might need to be more structured, but that sometimes sounds like a treat to me. I have had to be in charge of so many quadrants of my life and my children's lives that it would be a joy to simply *do what I am told*. For me, the perfect job would be to get paid to work for a smart boss who appreciates my talent and hard work. A bonus would be to be employed by a company that is socially conscious with merit-based benchmarks and California sunshine.

Occasionally, I catch myself enviously eyeing the cashier at Trader Joe's. Those *Fearless Flyer* employees always seem so jolly and so proud. It helps that Trader Joe's HR is fantastic, and a cashier job comes with real benefits, and the Trader Joe's brand is creative and impressive. I admire how those smart, sociable cashiers can swiftly scan your items while praising the caramelized porcini pizza they served at their party last night, and how the new *Panilonco* cabernet from Chile, at just $3.99 a bottle, was also a hit. It's a diverse and uplifting community and would be a nice, uncomplicated way to spend 40 hours a week being employed. It's likely that I wouldn't be great at this job, but every time I shop at Trader Joe's, I visualize myself wearing that festive Hawaiian shirt and belonging to a great team.

In all likelihood I won't become a cashier at Trader Joe's, but listening to my impulsive urges might help me narrow my search. Uttering this fantasy tells me that I want to work for a company with a product that makes me proud, with an employer who cares about their staff, and with workers who are happy to work. No fantasy job is too small or large. Yours might be Secretary of State, or surf shop owner, or Apple Genius Bar representative. Dream. Go big.

What do you love? What do you dream about?

One suggestion is to scan through your Google history for the last year. What places and people and adventures have you been most curious about? You may have forgotten, but Google has been keeping track. Also, become more aware of the gravitational pull in your daily routines. Make it your week's homework to focus on yourself and highlight what sparks your pleasure. Look around and notice when you say, "I could be happy doing that job."

This seemingly simple step is not always easy. Defining your cravings is a crucial step in finding work that will make you happy. So many of us fell into a job that was available and offered at the time. Now is your chance to define yourself. Please take this opportunity and list what gives you daily and weekly delight. You won't always get completely what you want in a job; however, knowing your pleasure points makes the job hunt a lot clearer. And will carve you into a more desirable candidate.

My Best Personality Test

Over the years, I have tried many versions of Personality Tests (both free and costly), highly recommended by life coaches, therapists, ethical evaluators, etc.; and while they could describe what I wanted to be, none of them had any staying power.

This past winter, my college-aged son was watching the new *Late Show* as Stephen Colbert asked, "*Who is the real Stephen Colbert?*" In a hilarious public plea of self-discovery, Stephen took the 16 Personalities Test on national TV. It was an entertaining television bit and has since created a calvacade of discovery for me, my family, and many friends.

16Personalites.com is the user-happy godchild of the more acclaimed Meyers Briggs Test and *for free* will ask you fifty or so snap questions and analyze your persona, including how your type tends to act as a parent, in their career, and in various roles in an organization.

Amused and curious, my son took the test. He was fascinated by the results and sent the link around to everyone he knew. It only takes eight minutes on your smartphone . . . and it's an easy blast. And the sharing has snowballed. I have never been one to follow my horoscope, I don't go to psychics, and I am often skeptical of most therapists, but 16personalities.com is an amazing first step in understanding yourself and your motivations. It succinctly described how my circuitry works best, and how those around me might excel, too. Recently, while away at a skating competition with my youngest daughter Billi's Syncro team, and over coffee with one mom, I casually mentioned how insightful the 16 Personality Test was for my family. After a speedy app download, within ten minutes, Bonnie was confirmed as the "Protagonist"; and before our dinner ended that evening, every single mom had taken the test as had nearly all their respective family members. Around the big table, fifty-seven new people had been given a complimentary moniker that described them each to a tee: The Campaigner, The General, The Debater, The Entrepreneur, The Consul, etc.

Not only is 16personalities.com an impressively insightful free test, it's an enjoyable ice-breaker. Taking the test alone or in a bonding group will thrust you into a contemplative mode as you all discover what makes you tick. I promise I wasn't paid to endorse 16personalities, but any self-discovery that can be fun and communal for the whole family is a solid win.

Extra Credit for Sale

Since I was so knocked out by these insights, I bought the Premium Profile and received over 160 pages of in-depth information about my archetype and how it reacts in the world with other types. This included a large section on careers and interpersonal relationships. I found what I learned invaluable. It was like taking a psychology class specifically catered for me. Although I bought into this site as research, it turned out to be quite perceptive and helpful to me as a communicator and potential job-searcher.

(http://personalitygrowth.com/the-late-night-show-with-stephen-colbert-does-15-minute-segment-on-myers-briggs/).

"Give a girl the right pair of shoes and she will conquer the world."
—Marilyn Monroe

Reveal Your Expertise; Come Out as a *Mom for Hire.*

In addition to discovering what you're passionate about, you need to figure out what you're actually *good* at. It's important to love your job, but you also want to be successful at it. And you want to make sure it's worth your financial while to head out to the office every (or most) days. Most often, the things we're good at tend to be more enjoyable. Pinpointing your strengths (and areas of challenge) will not only help you identify the right job, but will make you a more attractive candidate once you get into the interview phase (Step 6). For now, we're laying all the right groundwork so a) you're on track for the right opportunities and b) you're already as prepared as possible once those opportunities start to present themselves.

Today, let's think about past jobs, projects, and your role within your family and friend group. Everyone is an expert at something. What are you naturally good at?

- Are you particularly effective at *communicating* with a wide variety of people?
- Do you feel comfortable *negotiating* or holding firm once you've made a decision?
- Do people come to you for *advice*? About what subject?
- Are you more of a *creator* than an *executor*?
- Can you be a *salesman* for your own creation? Or *advocate* for others?

> " *Before 40, you wear your face . . .*
> *After 40, you wear your life on your face.* "
> —Grandmother Bessie, Yiddish proverb from Vilnius, Lithuania

Expert List

Proudly circle all your skills or talents on the "Expert List" below.

"I am an expert in . . ."

• Acting	• Guiding	• Planning
• Adapting	• Illustrating	• Preparing
• Advising	• Imagining	• Programming
• Analyzing	• Improvising	• Proofreading
• Anticipating	• Integrating	• Protecting
• Arguing	• Interpreting	• Recording
• Assembling	• Interviewing	• Representing
• Assisting	• Investigating	• Resolving
• Budgeting	• Judging	• Sewing
• Coaching	• Leading	• Sketching
• Composing	• Lecturing	• Speaking
• Consolidating	• Listening	• Styling
• Counseling	• Manipulating	• Supervising
• Creating	• Maintaining	• Taking Inventory
• Critiquing	• Mediating	• Teaching
• Curating	• Meeting	• Training
• Debating	• Memorizing	• Translating
• Designing	• Motivating	• Traveling
• Developing	• Navigating	• Trouble-shooting
• Discovering	• Negotiating	• Tutoring
• Distributing	• Operating	• Typing
• Editing	• Organizing	• Unifying
• Evaluating	• Overseeing	• Verbalizing
• Filing	• Painting	• Writing
• Finishing	• Piloting	• Other
• Founding	• Persuading	
• Giving	• Photographing	

*Extra copies available to print from DeborahJelinNewmyer.com

Specify the Parameters of Your Ideal Job:
What **Can** I Live Without? And What **Can't** . . .?

The Bureau of Labor of Statistics (2012) reports that the average worker holds 11.3 jobs over a career span and that women are unemployed for 25 percent of their career. Thus, conversations about job changes, especially for women, will happen several times throughout your life. A career needs to be seen in chapters; some transitions are rockier than others. No professional path is a direct line up a single ladder. In her book, *Lean In,* Sheryl Sandberg describes a person's career path as a multi-tiered "jungle gym" rather than a linear "ladder." Luckily, there are plenty of ways to get to the top and panoramic rewarding views along the way. Life is rarely linear, and the work you do throughout your life will change as you go. No longer is your career path decided in high school or college, and it is quite rare that the company you join right out of school will sustain you throughout your working life. Promotions, failures, reinventions—start-and-stop-and-start-again are the new normal. Get comfortable with change . . . it's a constant.

To a working mom, it often seems confounding just how "busy" a stay-at-home life can be. However unsettling it may be, sometimes a time-out from the working wheel is the best path to a new chapter. Likewise, it is equally bewildering to an off-ramped mom how many women could run a household and family and also work a full-time job. We all settle into our own forest and get used to our surrounding trees.

I have found that the best way to frame my time away from the work force—be it a three-month maternity leave or a longer step away—is to view it as the chance to regroup and ask myself crucial questions about what direction would be best for me.

If you are truly happy at home (and can afford to stay), please do. But if you want something else, anything is possible. This hour will take a comprehensive look at what you will do and what you won't do. Please take this hour to establish some solid parameters for your work/life plan. Let's start getting specific with some boundaries.

During this hour, you need to specify what you *will do* and what you *won't do.* It's time to gain clarity about your best-case job. As important as it is to uncover your ideal job, you equally need to draw a line in the sand as to what is "unacceptable" in a job. It will amaze you that once you answer these seemingly simple questions, you will weed out many tangential paths and increase your worth as an employee.

Reach-In Exercise: SPECIFY YOUR "MUST HAVES" AND "DON'T NEEDS" AND "WISDOM TO KNOW THE DIFFERENCE."

Direction: Old Job versus New Direction.

	Yes	No
Do I want to return to my paused profession?		
Do I need to keep amortizing my academic investments?		
Was I talented (enough) in my old field?		
Was I succeeding in my old job?		
Was it making me happy?		
Could I be more productive in a different field?		
Is the new *me* dreaming of a fresh start?		

Time Commitment: Part-time versus Full-time

	Yes	No
Am I ready to commit to a 9-to-5 job?		
Do I need a job with flexible hours?		
Am I willing to ask a potential employer for these hours?		
Can my mate free up some hours for childcare?		

Financial Needs: Paycheck versus Fulfillment

	Yes	No
Is the paycheck essential to my family's well-being?		
. . . Is that my primary reason for returning to work?		
Am I actually needed at home?		
Does being home give me enough happiness?		

Continued . . .

Do I need to be employed for emotional reasons? _____ _____

Environment: Cubicle versus Outdoors   Yes   No

Do I prefer to work:

    At a desk? _____ _____

    Behind a counter? _____ _____

    In a studio/factory? _____ _____

    With a team? _____ _____

    On my own? _____ _____

    With my hands? _____ _____

    On my feet? _____ _____

Location: Local versus Distant Places: Yes   No

Can I realistically travel for work? _____ _____

Do I want to be away from home? _____ _____

Does my family have any special needs that reduce my flexibility? _____ _____

For how many folks am I listed as the "in case of emergency"
    contact? Is this flexible? _____ _____

Who's In Charge? Driver versus Backseat: Yes   No

Do I want to be the boss or have a boss? _____ _____

Do I have access to start-up money? _____ _____

Do I want to go it alone or have a partner? _____ _____

Do I see myself in a corporate setting or an entrepreneurial realm? _____ _____

Can I manage in a family business where the pecking
    order may already be established? _____ _____

Company Core Values: Socially Conscious versus Money-Driven: Yes   No

How important are corporate women's issues
    (equal pay, maternity leave, etc.)? _____ _____

Can I work for a finance company that cares only about profit? _____ _____

Does the politics of the Administration and Board matter to me? _____ _____

Does the office need to have a "giving back" component? _____ _____

Does the company have a diverse hiring policy? _____ _____

Is the office environmentally conscious and sustainable? _____ _____

Are dogs allowed on the premises? _____ _____

What job boundaries can you embrace and what are deal-breakers?

Perhaps these questions feel remedial or tedious, but the more you can envision your future work boundaries and cravings, the easier it will be to brand yourself as a candidate who is ready to take the next step. The more assertive you are about defining your parameters, the more attractive a job candidate you become.

Why Women Want to Return

According to the most fascinating Hidden Brain Drain Task Force Study, the single most common reason for a woman wanting to reenter the work force (36 percent) was "to have a personal source of income." And the close second factor in returning was "career satisfaction." While many women cited a need to bolster their household's income, money alone wasn't enough "to prompt women to return." The 2009 study concluded that major motivating factors in moms wanting to on-ramp were to give back to society, make a positive contribution, work with interesting people, and solve interesting problems. It seems that many women want to return for the work itself. After off-ramping into motherhood, there seemed to be a switch in focus from "climbing the corporate ladder" to "wanting to feel good about themselves." Dramatically, the study found that only 9 percent of highly qualified women wanted to go back to the company they used to work for. Women with advanced law, business, academic, and medical degrees often needed to reanalyze their more adult craving to work and discover new paths.[1]

Reach-Out Exercise: ANNOUNCE YOUR READINESS FOR A NEW PROFESSIONAL CHAPTER!

Turn your percolating work-craving into an event. Maybe even host a celebratory party!

- Tell your mate.
- Tell all your friends.
- Tell your kids.
- Tell your parents.
- Tell every long-lost friend you run into.

---

[1] The Hidden Brain Drain Task Force. 2009 Questionnaire of a nationally representative group of 2,443 highly qualified woman and 653 of their male peers.

"Hear Ye. Hear Ye. I'm a **Mom for Hire!"**

You might be very surprised. Sometimes, the very act of letting people know you are looking might open up a job gate you never knew was there. Someone might need extra help at their stationery store on Main Street, or a consultant opportunity at your old firm might have just cropped up, or the market shifts and a bottom-drawer project suddenly becomes timely. Open your mouth and open your eyes. Look around. More likely, announcing your desire to go back to work is just the beginning of the search. But you have officially *started*. It may feel as though you are alone in your desire to "Job-Up," but many friends are searching, too.

Reach-Out Exercise: PROUDLY TELL ALL YOU'VE BECOME A *MOM FOR HIRE.*

Begin the chatter. Text, Instagram, announce in a newsletter that you are on the job prowl

- Make a toast at your next birthday party.
- Send out a "friends" email letting people know you're on your way to something new, big, and fabulous. And post a "changed" status on your facebook page.
- Reconnect with at least one key person at your old job.
- Let your world know that you are READY.

If you ask for input, everybody will have opinions and advice, and maybe even a real lead. If you have been insulated in your mom cocoon, emerge. Start hatching. A sense of community will happen if you reach out and broadcast your shift. You will discover that you are not alone. As you declare that you want something more, you can inspire and motivate others to look at you differently. You have started.

" *There are only two mistakes one can make along the road to truth; not going all the way, and not starting.* "
—Buddha

Step Two

GET ORGANIZED AND FIND YOUR NETWORK

Okay, now that you've told everyone you want to go back to work, there is no turning back. Own it. You're on your way! As you climb these steps, you will become fortified with a solid organizational system, a snazzy categorized list of friends and peers, and a fear-blasting readiness test. You are getting prepared and psyched to start the job of finding a job.

We all remember our first day back to school, or that New Year's Day crossfit class. It may hurt a little, you might be sore and wiped out, but tomorrow will be a little easier, and soon you will have developed a strong work habit muscle. So on we go!

"*If a guitar sits for too long, it's not tuned.*"
—Ruthanne Huvane, casting executive

Hour Goals

Hour One:	**Create** a Next Chapter office.
Hour Two:	**Commit** to an organizing system.
Hour Three:	**List** your network of friends and acquaintances.
Hour Four:	**Categorize** those networks into focus groups of support.
Hour Five:	**Test** your readiness.

Hour One
Create a Mom For Hire Office

While last week you claimed a "ME" hour to focus on finding a Next Chapter, today let's designate an alluring "ME" space and claim that space as your Next Chapter office. It's important that each time you sit down to work at becoming a *Mom for Hire*, you make a ritual of returning to a spot that's all yours.

For me, through my forty years spent at twelve different jobs, I'd inhabited several office spaces. However, I had never written a book before, so my noise and focus needs were somewhat persnickety. Luckily, my home was empty for much of the day, and my chair fit perfectly underneath an idle banquette in a rarely used living room. I had a laptop, bought a few pens and an accordion folder, cleared off a few bookshelves . . . and my office was made.

Reach-Out Exercise: CREATE A MOM FOR HIRE OFFICE NEST.

You can head to your local stationery store, or you can order everything with one click online. I am pretty old-school and prefer to print and touch and file my work. Plus, it's fun to set up a designated space to work in. But if your brain is cyberproficient, you could get away with 1) this workbook, 2) your laptop (or even a smartphone), and 3) a few colored pens. Honestly, you could probably raid your kid's bottom drawer and repossess his or her extra school supplies to fill your desk. However, to make this *Moms for Hire* commitment stick, you need to take ownership of a spot as your Next Chapter space, a zone where you can focus on these steps. Here's a specific, simple list of items you might find useful in creating your office:

Shopping List for a Simpliest Instant Office:
- ❏ Folders! You don't need a whole filing cabinet; an accordion file is plenty.
- ❏ Highlighters in assorted colors; you'll use these later. Or colored pens.
- ❏ Nice stock paper to write and rewrite your résumé.
- ❏ Cover letter stationary and envelopes.
- ❏ A label-maker if you don't have one already.
- ❏ Office supply upkeep: ink, pens/pencils, stapler, scissors, printer paper, Post-it notes.

Your Portable Office

If private real estate is not available at home, try carving out a productive "MY" place wherever you can focus for at least one hour at a time. It is a thing of legend that the first Harry Potter was written in an Edinburgh, Scotland, coffee shop. And although it wasn't always ideal, much of *Moms for Hire* was worked through at eight different Le Pain Quotidiens in Los Angeles and New York City, I did most of my research at my son's high school desk that has the best Internet in the house, and the rest at the El Segundo Skating Rink tables overlooking my daughter's three-hour practices, and occasionally in our lovely public library. Even though I had a designated space of my own at home, for various reasons, I often worked on-the-go.

Most important, you need to find a "Me Zone" for your habitual daily hour. That space could be a quiet portion of your home or it could travel with this book; *Moms for Hire* can become your traveling office. If you need to streamline your hour into a portable office, grab this book in a designated tote bag, add your daily planner or calendar app, a few colored pens, and a light laptop (don't forget the correct charger!). You will need access to a real computer for some of the list-making steps, but many of the worksheets and exercises are within this book. Also, many of the reach-out steps are practical and out-in-the-world exercises.

Daily Do List

❑ Created my *Moms for Hire* office zone.

❑ Scheduled a visit to the office zone every day, for an hour.

❑ Took a trip to Staples, Amazon one-clicked, or gathered extra supplies to officially claim *Mom for Hire* zone.

Hour Two
Commit to a Daily Organizing as Your New BFF

Note of Disclosure: I do not pretend to be a Pew researcher, and *Moms for Hire* is not a PhD dissertation or data-rich statistical study. Most of my knowledge comes from over forty years of curiously listening and the sixty-plus conversational interviews I conducted with all sorts of moms over the course of writing this book. Please think of *Moms for Hire* as upbeat advice from your bossy (caring) girlfriend.

After scores of conversations with prominent, highly capable women, I discovered the most consistent route to success was their hearty ability to *get and remain organized*. Not an absolute truth, but in general, a messy home equals a messy mind.

Woman for woman, I heard the same tried-and-true system for being productive: *list* and *prioritize* the components of a project, then *follow through* in a specified order. Simplistic as it may seem, being organized is what seemed to divide those who efficiently accomplish great things and those who do not. Some are born with organizational instincts; others have to work at being logistic and administrative every day. Having an organized life may not come naturally, but it can be learned. Grit and determination are a matter of willpower; you can push yourself to start cleaning out your life and making room for something new, like, say . . . a career!

In every interview, I asked, "What tools did you use to keep a calendar and to-do list? How do you stay on track?" To my surprise, even the most computer-savvy women responded with an old-school answer: WRITE IT DOWN. While most have given up their Rolodex for smartphone digital contacts, for calendar and to-do lists, the old-school Filofax is still solidly in the mix. Many of us rely on the less leathery "At-A-Glance" calendar/planner. Even women who are smarter than their smartphones, and executives with a great team of assistants, keep themselves organized with their own pen and a hard copy calendar to keep track of their day.

Nothing beats writing it down.

Go ahead and ask your productive friends how they keep themselves organized. Visit them at their home or office. What calendar system do they use? How do they remind themselves of tasks to be undertaken? What kind of to-do list system do they employ?

When I polled my most together friends, they revealed they:

- Always have paper and pen nearby so they can write down notes and reminders.
- Always keep a running to-do list.
- Always straighten up their own desk before leaving for the day.
- Always make their own bed in the morning.
- Always clean their sink and tidy their kitchen at night.
- Constantly update the large family calendar in the kitchen.
- Always ask everyone they know for their favorite organizational tips.

Getting and staying organized requires two things: First, you need to actively psych yourself into a happy cleaning mood. Then, you will need to turn that neatening-up system into a daily habit. There are several books out there about organization that delve into great detail about the hows and whys of decluttering and organizing. I will keep it simple here: suffice it to say, having the innards of your home, car, and workspace neat and tidy is a HUGE deal. It reflects your inner clarity.

It's easy to get used to ignoring those overstuffed back shelves while pulling your outfit from that towering pile of sweatpants, but, like doing your own sit-ups, closet-purging is nobody's favorite task. And it is not a task you can easily delegate. For many, editing out the old is personal and painful and thus is often relegated to the I'll-get-to-it-later pile . . . in another galaxy. That being said, you might want to have a friend over to help you say "bye-bye" to your eighties and nineties power suits.

Reach-Out Exercise: ASK AN EXPERT HOW THEY DO IT.

I recommend a reconnaissance date with one or two of your most productive friends to ask them how—specifically—they keep themselves organized and fit. Visit them at their home or office, witness and copy some of their arranging habits.

- What calendar system do they use?
- How do they order and remind themselves of tasks to be undertaken?
- What kind of to-do list system do they employ?
- How do they organize their old paperwork and files, their desktop icons, their old suits?
- How do they dispose of their excess things? Do they have a giveaway system?

You might need to get some organizing supplies, but mostly just large trash bags for, well, trash (and donations).

Once you determine you are ready to get organized, spark your mood by playing fun music and begin the cleanse. Today, you will clean out a single space. Dedicate the next hour to organizing just ONE closet, ONE cabinet in your house, or ONE outgrown bookshelf. It could be the hall linens, the kitchen junk drawer, the broom closet, or your shoes. Pick a sector, any cluttered sector, and begin a habit of cleaning every day.

When I cleaned out my bedroom closet, I found three entire drawers of panty hose. Fifteen-years'-worth: sandal-toes to control-tops; pregnancy hose to Valentine's Day silks; skin-toned to every version of black hose and nostalgic fishnets. Suddenly, I remembered that I live in southern California and only need to wear stockings four times a year. Tops. I became furious at the realization that three of my eight drawers were occupied with extinct items. Throw them away!

Some people find they need a glass of wine or nostalgic music or a friend's editing eye to get in the mood. You may need to hire a professional to insistently coax you to finally throw away those years of holiday cards, or to remind you that your youngest child is fourteen and hasn't shopped at Gap Kids since she was ten. If you need to hire someone harsh to help you throw away your clutter, it is worth the expense to get this done. Consult Yelp or the National Association of Professional Organizers. There is plenty of help out there.

Reach-Out Exercise: HOW TO STOP PROCRASTINATING.

If procrastination is your glitch, there are apps, books, and websites to help keep you on track and continue on an efficient path back to work. My most effective route to getting things done is to devote five minutes every night to creating a to-do list for tomorrow. When the morning begins, and you are ready to be productive . . .

- Put your phone away.
- Set a goal for the day.
- Break that goal into smaller, "accomplishable" tasks.
- Schedule each task for a specific time. (Set time prompt on your smartphone.)
- When your reminder dings, focus on that single task.
- Give yourself credit for completing each task and enjoy the feeling of accomplishment when you check off that task.

Continued . . .

- Reward yourself with something you love—take a walk in nature, watch lousy TV . . . whatever you want.
- Get as far as possible without killing yourself in the process—even if you are slow. . . . Keep moving forward.
- Do your best. And be okay with your best.

Reach-Out Exercise: TOTAL ORGANIZATION LEADS TO MAXIMUM FLEXIBILITY.

Spend some time today going through a few organizational systems, and find a calendar and a to-do tool that works for you. Truthfully, you need to surf around and find the listing and scheduling tool that work best for you. It could be a hard paper or digital resource. Just pick an organizational system and make it an easy habit.

"If you make your bed every morning you will have accomplished the first task of the day. It will give you a small sense of pride and it will encourage you to do another task and another and another."
—Admiral William McRaven, 2014 Commencement Address, U of Texas

How Did SHE Do It?
Total organization leads to maximum flexibility.
Kathleen K., mother of two teenage daughters, movie producer, and executive

Kathy grew up in a small town in Northern California. Her dad was a very smart local lawyer; her mom was even smarter and a mother of three fun girls. After Kathy's

Continued . . .

graduation from a State School in San Diego, she gravitated to Los Angeles, got a job as an assistant, worked tirelessly, saved her money, and always made herself vital to every boss she ever had.

Before long, *Kathy the assistant* had become *Kathy the producer* for her boss Steven Spielberg, and over the last 40 years she's never stopped working hard and proving herself to be one of the top movie producers of all time. Kathy did so many things right: she married well, she's raised two wonderful daughters, and she was always a high-spirited, resourceful, impact player.

Even now, as she oversees Lucasfilm Ltd. and the entire Star Wars Enterprise, no task is too small or too large, and she derives her greatest pride by getting the job done. Somehow, she never finds the time to either complain or to boast about any of it.

While there is a bounty of helpful advice with which Kathy has imbued me about leadership, ambition, and manning your own intentions, I was always gobsmacked by her organizational command. Clutter and dust roll off her.

For Kathy, keeping her office, her car, and her life spic-and-span was always instinctual. But for many of us, we've slackened our grip on an arranged desktop, an efficient schedule, and a prioritized mind. As our daily life cells divided with parenting, sustaining an ordered life became impossible. Not for Kath. And although she is not capable of bragging about her organizational systems, here are just a few aspirational habits of Kathy's that I have seen and envied in action:

- *Only touch a piece of paper once:* Read it, deal with it and be done. Emails, too.
- *Before exiting your car, spend an extra 45 seconds tidying up:* Gather your trash, put your sunglasses back in their case, and bring order to your stuff. You never know who might need a lift to your next meeting.
- *Always have a small, ready-to-go fanny pack assembled:* Stashed with an ID or passport, a credit card, a charger, some cash, and maybe a toothbrush. You never know when you will have to run to the airport and convince a plane and pilot to fly your entire cast and crew of *Jurassic Park* off the island after a Class 5 Hurricane. Or simply when your friend's stranded by the side of the road in Fresno.
- *Purge all your closets and quadrants regularly:* Never buy anything new until you've given something away. Your closet and your little sister will smile upon you.

Clutter Clean Wednesdays

Everyone wants to be more productive. We all want less belly fat. We all want to waste less and never lose our reading glasses. Creating small rituals helps. If you want to improve your balance, stand on one foot while your brush your teeth. If you want to strengthen your pelvic power, do your Kegels every time you ride up an elevator. There's a popular new weekly ritual of Throwback Thursdays: some people develop the habit of adding a nostalgic picture to their Instagram or Facebook page every Thursday. My scattered family never misses a Sunday night dinner gathering, and watching *Survivor* together in real-time is our cozy Wednesday ritual.

This week, start a new tradition of "Clutter Clean Wednesday." When the mid-week comes around, put aside, or even schedule, a half an hour to purge and clean one specific space. Every Wednesday. One over-stuffed purse. One hall closet. One electronic cord and charger collection. One photo album. Every Wednesday. One small thing. Make it a habit. Make it a ritual.

Daily Do List

❑ Committed to a specific calendar and to-do list system.

❑ Looked through various organizational websites and/or books.

❑ Cleaned out one closet, one junky desk drawer, one photo file, etc.

❑ Activated one new habit for productivity.

A Word About Your Daily Do List.

At the conclusion of every hour of exercise, you've probably noticed that I list a few items you may have accomplished today. Each one of these cumulative exercises is designed to nudge you closer to a happy profession. If you skip a few, that's fine. If you go beyond these proposed exercises, that's great, too. What is most important is that you honor your day's accomplishments, and that you habitually begin to write down and check in with your own "Intentions and Accomplishments." You are welcomed to rely on my prompts, or go your own way with your own organizational system. Eventually, this guidebook will be completed, and you will be on your own. So get ready for your eventual, solo To-Do List habit.

Hour Three
Generate Your Network of Professional and Personal Supporters

"I actually have everything I need, I just can't always seem to find it."
—Me, Deb Newmyer

The best way to land a job is through a referral. Period. Ya' gotta know somebody. Or even know somebody who knows somebody.

And while it may seem that in today's competitive job market, your age and doubled-up priorities might become a demerit, in fact there are many hidden pluses to your adult, diversified status. You now know more people and more things, and the bigger your database is . . . the better your network can be. I will bet you've forgotten a majority of your helpful connections. Time to refresh your list. The older we get, the more *somebodies* we know (or once knew). And once you are ready to smartly ask those *somebodies* for specific help . . . those friends beget colleagues.

Your broad spectrum of acquaintances can open doors to an equally broad spectrum of jobs. Those acquaintances are your surest bet for getting your foot in any given office door. Every employer prefers a referral from someone she trusts! Think about it: If you were hiring a new baby-sitter, would you rather scroll through unfamiliar applicants on Craigslist or hire the woman your neighbor can't stop raving about? If someone refers you for a job (or even a preliminary interview), you've left a good first impression before you even walk through the door. Cha-ching!

Reach-In: TAKE STOCK OF YOUR CIRCLE OF COLLEAGUES.

Today, we're going to refresh your circle-of-friends list, the inventory of your allies and acquaintances. One of the perks of being a thirty-plus-year-old grown-up is that you know a lot of people. Once you begin retracing for potential supporters, there will be scores of people you have forgotten you know. Thank goodness the Internet has been keeping track for you.

Think broadly. Keep your circles wide and think of all possible networks. You're trying to gather names of people who might be able to contribute to your job hunt in a positive or constructive way. Whether they help, inspire, conspire, headhunt, connect,

Continued . . .

brainstorm, or advocate, these women (or men!) might end up opening doors you didn't even know existed. Go to your social media pages: I am not sure if this is a worthy brag, but I have 1,006 Facebook friends and 386 LinkedIn connections. With a ten-minute effort this week, I could double those contacts.

For today's hour, pull out your aged Rolodex, your school roster, or your holiday card mailing list, and scroll through all your contacts. Perhaps you can "refind" that parent on your kids' sports teams list, or a coffee pal from an extension class you took two years ago, or familiar faces at the gym, or an old classmate you reconnected with at a reunion, or friendly local business owners. Every one of these random connections can become your job hunting network. Remember: think broadly!

Your Personalized Focus Group

Female Peers—List friends you are comfortable asking for help:

_____	_____	_____
_____	_____	_____
_____	_____	_____
_____	_____	_____
_____	_____	_____
_____	_____	_____

- *Which ones are mothers?*
- *Who is working full-time?*
- *Are they self-employed? Artists . . . entrepreneurs?*
- *How many took time off? For how long?*
- *Who successfully on-ramped back into ANY job?*
- *What was their on-ramp path?*

Male Contacts with Connections (likely they never sidetracked their career for the Homefront):

_____   _____   _____

Women You Know Who Have Succeeded in the Workplace—Might feel beyond your reach, but you'll need to reach (a.k.a. Your Fantasy Mentors):

_____   _____   _____

_____   _____   _____

_____   _____   _____

_____   _____   _____

_____   _____   _____

_____   _____   _____

This is Your Envy List/Fantasy Mentor List. No shame here. We all have those women we compare ourselves to—it's human nature. While you definitely don't want to allow toxicity or negative energy into your *Mom for Hire* space, writing out a list of the women you envy or admire can help you identify your priorities and, if used appropriately, can fuel your job quest. T___ can be people you know or don't know, TV personalities, or corporate giants.

Now ___onest, what part of her success do you most covet?

- ___'s got financial freedom.
- ___e's got a high-profile status.
- ___he gets to be part of a grown-up office culture.
- She's following HER passion.
- She has a great boss who compliments her work.
- She *is* the boss.
- She works her own hours and creates her own art.
- She's got office and occupational cred.
- Her spouse is supportive.
- Her spouse is impressed with her.

As you create your list of people you know, begin to envision this group as your village, your network. Begin to own your connections. Let your envy of their good stature fuel your quest for gratifying work. There is still plenty of time. Your next chapter is waiting for you to make it happen. Let's go.

How Did SHE Do It?
Without shame, she left her perch. And then, without shame, she returned.

Lisa F., mother of four, Corporate Lawyer and Strategist, NYC

I first met Lisa through my television set. She was being interviewed by Lesley Stahl on *60 Minutes* as an example of a career-oriented woman who chose to opt out. Lisa had been President of the *Stanford Law Review*, clerked for Supreme Court Justice Ruth Bader Ginsburg, and was racing up the legal-star track at a Fortune 500. After Lisa got married and began having children, and her husband began an intense surgical residency, they decided that she would step away from her high-powered firm to raise their kids. Lesley was surprised by the decision, as were many viewers.

A full decade later, Lisa was eager to return to full-time work, and she was interested in learning about business and how one grows a company. She still had the same brainpower and guts and enthusiasm for challenges, and believed that running a household, raising children, and working for non-profits had taught her how to get things done, with all deliberate speed.

Although she may have looked like a traditional housewife, Lisa remained active in women's rights and reproductive rights, doing advocacy work for Planned Parenthood. She kept up with her professional contacts and forged new ones. One New Year's Eve, Lisa made a resolution to give herself six months to explore a variety of jobs, turn on her *Mom for Hire* switch, and pursue positions that interested her. She met with hundreds of people, bracing herself for snide comments about having no long-term experience, and felt fortunate to emerge with several offers. Employers were understanding of her personal choices, and many were willing to take a chance on a smart and fearless woman. She chose an opportunity to work for a business that allowed her not just to oversee a legal department, but to be a part of the leadership team, and be involved in all strategic decisions.

Today, Lisa is Chief of Strategy and Chief Legal Officer at a large luxury retail company. She has found a job she likes, at an organization that respects her, and is in sync with her notions of family balance. Of course, she cannot help but wonder what she might have achieved professionally had she remained in the realm of her elite lawyer peers; two of her colleagues were on the short list for the Supreme Court . . . But she's happy for the opportunity to have been so involved in her children's upbringing—she considers it a gift—and is deeply proud of them. Lisa made a choice that came with clear career sacrifices, but she's chosen to always look forward and avoid feelings of regret.

" I think a lot of people dream . . . And while they are busy dreaming, the really happy people, the really successful people, the really engaged, powerful people, are busy doing. "
—Shonda Rhimes

<u>**Daily Do List**</u>

❏ Created my list of friends and acquaintances.

❏ Wrote my role model-mentor-envy list.

❏ Kept up with my organizing and cleaned ONE junk space.

Hour Four
Categorize Your Network into Focus Groups

Now that you have created a master list of all your potential allies and associates, let's spend the next hour breaking them into helpful camps. Once you categorize these connections, you will have several useful networks to refer to during the upcoming stages of your job hunt.

One connection might be the perfect person to take out to lunch because she just got her real estate license after her youngest started high school. For her, this journey is still fresh and memorable, so picking her brain and hearing her story could be an encouraging step. Another person might be a recruiter for an Internet company; he's got NO job for you and only has a few rushed minutes for advice. Grab those minutes he's offering and soak up as much information as he can offer. A college suitemate works in Human Resources at a large agency . . . You know you want to work in the corporate world, but you have no idea what *kind* of job you want. You might want to save that meeting until your "ask" is more succinct. So, put that friend on a "Future Resource" list.

Reach-In Exercise: CATEGORIZE YOUR ACQUAINTANCES AND ALLIES.

Take a look at your list and begin to write out categories that best describe your friend groupings. While it is interesting to identify which moms work, which are stay-at-homers, which of your friends are not parents, and which moms on-ramped, for this exercise it is probably most useful to divide your master list into categories according to how they might help link you to your next career chapter.

- Fellow Job Hunters—Create mutual support group, only a phone call away.

  _____   _____

  _____   _____

- Working Moms—Willing to meet and talk about her path.

  _____   _____

  _____   _____

Continued . . .

- Friends Who Know About Job Market (and maybe Jobs)—Willing to meet.

  _____   _____

  _____   _____

- Recruiters/Headhunters/Job Experts—Willing to advise.

  _____   _____

  _____   _____

- Specific Person or Group without Job Opening—Informational meeting.

  _____   _____

  _____   _____

- Specific Connection or Company with Job Opening—Gear up to get hired.

  _____   _____

  _____   _____

You don't need a million categories, and the same name can appear in more than one. Within each category, take two highlighters and use one color to mark the friends you think could actively help you right now, and another color for friends who could help you down the line. Also notice if there seem to be glaringly obvious categories with no names under them; perhaps you need to widen your circle—put on your big girl pants and meet some new people. If it's been a while since you've oiled up the schmooze machine, don't worry; it will get easier. It might feel at first like you're slurring your words and can't complete a sentence with nouns and verbs in their proper places, but trust me, it gets easier.

Never Forget an Ally.

Finding a job could easily take months, and along the way plenty of people will be on your side. I found it very helpful to keep track of the folks who I reached out to and contributed to my job quest. To keep me organized and ready to thank them when my goal was reached, I kept a log that gave me a valuable history of my job-hunting path. Hopefully you will, too.

Contacts & Connections			
Who You Know	What's Your "Ask"?	Date You Reached Out	Date to Follow Up

*Extra copies available to print from DeborahJelinNewmyer.com

*" If you want to get a job, every day you need to find **three**
new friends online . . . send **three** new emails . . . reach
out with **three** new phone calls. "*
—Amy Coleman, freelance producer

One easy method for keeping on top of past, present, and future networking lists is to commit to finding and adding five new Facebook or LinkedIn friends a week. The great news about those friendly sites is that they encourage you to keep seeking new connections and they keep track for you—your circle is stored and updated regularly.

Daily Do List

❏ Categorized my allies and acquaintance list.

❏ Went back to my wells for more potential assists.

❏ Kept a log of all my reaches.

Hour Five
Find Your Readiness; Find Your Hours

As a mother and homekeeper, you've had to become a flexible and efficient multitasker. My guess is that your biggest challenge is claiming time for yourself. It feels somehow greedy to consider yourself a priority when there is *always* someone else whose needs seem more immediate and whose skills seem less capable. Wrong, wrong. As mother, many of us find ourselves in the conventional rut of being the chef, the chauffeur, the social secretary, the plumber, the toast-to-a-golden-brown expert, the button-sewer-on-er, the therapist, and the 24/7 on-call ER doctor. In service to others, you've neglected yourself. Now is the time to start striking a fair and healthy balance.

Everybody wants to be more productive, but achievements can be elusive, especially if you have been in stay-at-home mode for a while. You've dropped your last kid off at school, you've done the morning chitchat with the other moms, you're running low on printer paper and frozen fruit (because your son will only eat his veggies blended into a smoothie), your daughter has an orthodontist appointment at 2 p.m., and you know there's more on the never-ending to-do list, but you can't seem to pull it out of the recesses of your brain. You could always check in with your mom or sweat through spin class—there is always plenty to distract—being "busy" can take up a whole day.

Efficiency requires discipline, focus, and sometimes caffeine. One of the most often-used excuses for not finding a job is that you *don't have the time*. At this juncture, that excuse might be a fact. But if you truly want to find a job, let's use this step to *find* the time. The hours are there; you just have to be willing to carve them out for *yourself*. This step is designed to find those hours in your day you didn't know you had.

Reach-In: WHERE DO MY HOURS GO?

If you are NOT employed in the 9-to-5/40-hour-a-week conventional realm, you are often busy doing I'm not sure what. The "Do I know how to use my time productively?" question can only be answered by actually breaking it down and keeping a time log, which is why you diligently kept track of your hours last week (right?). Today, grab that Hour Log from Step One, pull out your highlighters, and tally up your hours.

Hour Log

How Many Hours Did You Spend On:

Home Maintenance: _____

Kids & Family: _____

Fitness & Beauty: _____

Volunteer/Training: _____

Speculative Work: _____

Compensated Work: _____

Free Time: _____

Once you have chronicled your typical week (hopefully it was not the first week of school, or Thanksgiving, or when your mate was out of town), you can start to divide these hours into 1) must-do hours, 2) can-delegate hours, and 3) "shiftable" hours. Sit with your weekly planner and your hourly log breakdown from Step One and be honest about all your weekly commitments and weekly pleasures. Circle your *fixed responsibilities*; these are all the hours you cannot reschedule or give away. But suddenly pockets of available hours will appear. For now, these hours may seem too random and sporadic to be job-worthy, but you found *some* hours. With a little effort, we can reroute those blocks of time into rewarding work. Even though you don't yet know what your new job will be, you need to understand your schedule and how that job will fit into it. The job you choose to seek will be determined by how much time you can actually afford to devote to it.

Optional Exercise: **Your Ideal Rendering of Your Weekly Schedule.**
Here's another blank weekly log breakdown. Neatly fill in only your most mandatory fixed "Mom Hours." Now, look at the hours you've successfully freed up! How much time is it? Honestly assess whether those hours can be shifted some more, and how you might be able to bundle these piecemealed hours into usable chunks of work time.

Hour Log, week of: _____

	Mon.	Tues.	Weds.	Thurs.	Fri.
6am					
7am					
8am					
9am					
10am					
11am					
noon					
1pm					
2pm					
3pm					
4pm					
5pm					
6pm					
7pm					
8pm					
9pm					
10pm					
11pm					

◼ Home   ◼ Kids/Family   ◼ Fitness & Beauty   ◼ Volunteer/Training/Spec   ◼ Compensated Work   ◼ Free Time

If you'd like to download extra log pages, go to my website DeborahJelinNewmyer.com and follow the link to Bonus Giveaways/Worksheets.

Reach-In Exercise: MEASURE YOUR READINESS.

There are so many positive aspects of being a stay-at-home mom. For me, I relish the pleasure of free daytime: the 8:25 a.m. relaxation time with a second cup of coffee, gardening in the daylight, an option for a noon yoga class, giving tours at my son's school, watching my daughter take her first step and master her first axel, a ladies' lunch. Those are my really sweet perks. Yet, I am willing to give up these perks for a satisfying career.

Are you?

While I truly enjoy my mom moments and precious freedoms, I equally want to feel more connected to the working world and a paycheck. I know I cannot have it all. However, if you take this test and determine you are currently fulfilled on this scenic mother route, be that person with pride. For now, if your life-work balance works for you—oh, happy day! Going back to work is not for everyone, and that truth is okay too. You can set this book aside for a time and perhaps revisit it in years to come.

Being appreciative and being grateful is a muscle. And within the psychology of our busy, caring-for-others day, rarely do any of us stop to acknowledge and announce the delights of our sunny moments. Every day, you need to strengthen your appreciation muscle or it will atrophy.

What pieces of your mom day do you most look forward to? List three of your guilty (or not so guilty) pleasures of being a stay-at-home mom:

1. _____

2. _____

3. _____

What are your weekly must-do priorities (childcare, groceries, house maintenance, etc.)?

Priorities: Hours Per Week:

_____

_____

_____

Continued . . .

What are the "treats" of your week that would be a big challenge to give up (e.g., coaching soccer, practicing piano, volunteering at a help line)?

Pleasures: Hours Per Week:

_____

_____

_____

What are the "treats" of your week that constitute pure "me" time (e.g., your manicure or book club)?

Priorities: Hours Per Week:

_____

_____

_____

What Would You Miss If You Went Back to Work?

We are all creatures of habit. Change is usually a little scary, and I'm sure this section has you in some knots over what's about to happen. Breathe. The goal is finding a killer job, and you will get there. Understandably, some fears might be coming up for you about what you might miss if you devote those hours to working. Spend a little time now being honest about those concerns.

Reach-In Exercise: DO YOU HAVE THE WILL TO RETURN TO WORK?

You'll notice that you can answer "Yes!" or "Oy!" to the following questions. Note that "Oy" is a response to a question that touches a part of you that you'd rather not see, but know is true. C'mon, sister. Dive in.

Question	Yes versus Oy		
Do you feel validated by the "calling" of being a stay-at-home mom?	Yes	or	Oy
Are you really *too* busy to look for work (or just afraid)?	Yes	or	Oy
Do you feel bewildered professionally (and paralyzed by confusion)?	Yes	or	Oy
Do you honestly believe your kids cannot manage without you?	Yes	or	Oy
Do you feel pressure from your mate to remain the homemaker?	Yes	or	Oy
Do you complain too much about what you don't have?	Yes	or	Oy
Do you complain about what you *do* have?	Yes	or	Oy
Do you think you'll be jumping ship if you have a job?	Yes	or	Oy
Are you burned out with parenting?	Yes	or	Oy
Do you still engage and enjoy the kids the way you used to or have you checked out emotionally?	Yes	or	Oy
Are you perhaps being a drama queen, and too often feeling victimized?	Yes	or	Oy

Get real. These questions are important. Whether you decide to stay-at-home or try to jump into working, you need to honestly reflect on your situation.

Daily Do List

❑ Charted my hours.

❑ Reworked my hours to free up time.

❑ Honestly appraised my readiness factor.

"Multi-tasking is my most powerful muscle source . . . Way stronger than my brain and vagina!"
—Alexandra Wentworth, Comedian & Author

Step Three
DECLUTTER YOURSELF

" I am having a crisis of confidence, and it's taking all my time. "
—Alicia Florrick, from *The Good Wife*

Forward onto Step Three! Your mission this week is to use these hours for some career speed-therapy. According to the most data-based back-to-work studies, the most successful job hunters are the folks who become "attractive candidates." Having a great résumé helps, and an excellent cover letter is important. And of course you will need a few positive recommendations, and some sort of inside track to clinch it. But all the headhunters in the world can't get you a job unless you present yourself as worthy and interesting.

The *most* attractive candidates—and the ones who win the job—are the job seekers who have done their homework. They know what they want, and they have unpacked their professional baggage. When it comes time to interview, if you carry that baggage into the office with you, you've already shot yourself in the foot.

In Step Three, you will admit to, and mend, a few of the psychological fences you have been bumping up against. Listen, we've all got quirks that make us less attractive to a boss. This week, you'll face-and-fix yours. These hours will help you get clarity on *why* you are unhappy when it comes to a career, or lack of one. You'll reach in and work through the reasons your career may have gone off-track.

There are a variety of moms out there, and many versions of traumatic job experiences. Some of us have been out of the job world for years. Some of us are job veterans and feel stuck in the rut of unfulfilling work. Some of us have never worked. Some left voluntarily, while others feel their job was taken away from them. This week is about dealing with the emotional gridlock of "*What pushed me off the work wheel?*"

Hour Goals

Hour One:	**Tell** your *Exit Story*.
Hour Two:	**Voice** a *Regret Testimony*.
Hour Three:	**Reach out** to your circle and support groups.
Hour Four:	**Give** value to your working-life memories.
Hour Five:	**Clean** the slate; uncover the unshackled "you."

I promise, you are not alone. The school's carpool lane is strewn with a long line of compromised careers.

Every mom is consulting their Filofax or iPhone, prioritizing all those reminders to return those too-small jammies to Target, orthodontist appointments, and then doubling back to the lacrosse field to pick up that forgotten stick. In another incarnation, your afternoon list would include paychecks, lunch meetings, other grown ups, and maybe a corner office.

You remember a time when your first thoughts related to your autonomy, ambitions, and accomplishments. Instead, you stepped off the career track, and now your biggest concern is whether the organic gummy bears have too much sugar in them. You are squinting to find a focus that helps foster independence. Not every second of every day, but, maybe more often than not lately, you find yourself thinking you want to recapture the positive feelings and circumstances surrounding your career.

Sometimes, the only way to move forward is to look back.

"Thirty-five percent of the female, college-educated workforce takes a family-induced off-ramp for an average of two-point-five years."
—Sylvia Anne Hewlett, *Off-Ramps and On-Ramps Revisited*

Exiting the Work Wagon

What was Your Reason for Exiting the Work Wagon?

- A medical emergency shifted you back home.
- You wanted to be a full-time mom.
- Your spouse was making more money, so you became the "home-stayer."
- You needed to change locations and move across the state/country.
- Your child had a special need or a special talent that required much of your time.
- Your parent or sibling was ailing.
- You felt unappreciated at work.
- You felt stressed that you were not being a good enough mother or employee.
- You lost your alpha drive.
- You were burned out at work.

Hour One
Tell Your Exit Story

Many exit stories were driven by a family member's *need* that pulled you off the work ramp. Also, much of motherhood and marital satisfaction is nestled in the happy truth that we are *needed*. But that pride of being needed only gets you so far. Eventually, you might yearn for a sense of work accomplishment that goes beyond your caretaking accomplishments. You might find yourself *having* a need that only a formal occupation with monetary compensation can fulfill. From now on, let your own ambition out of its mothering closet.

I've written my Exit Drama for you as a sisterly prompt for this exercise. If there is some other form of expression that feels more truthful and cathartic for you, by all means, use that! Write it, paint it, sing it, draw it—whatever will help you get it out of your head.

> **"*Life is made up of hard work and fitting into society.*"**
> —My mother's mantra

DEB'S EXIT STORY

As was expected, I always, always had a job, from age fourteen onward. Various jobs, but by age twenty-three, I was on a career path in the entertainment business. And by twenty-six, I had a job I loved for Steven Spielberg's Amblin Entertainment that lasted thirteen years. In the midst of that big career job, I got married and had three children. With each child I took a brief maternity leave and delegated much of my parenting and personal life to better-qualified help. For me, mothering my babies was easier after they had been burped and bathed by a more infant-centric nanny. I would come in for the glory: the bedtime story and cuddle. For years, my little secret was that parenting little ones was more difficult than mothering writers, directors, and talent. For over a decade, it was a very satisfying life. I was proud of my work, my marriage, and my children. I loved juggling all those elements.

During those alpha years, self-reflection was not in my bandwidth. I never paused to reflect on the cracks in my life. I simply proceeded, proudly "having it all," never considering there was a better balance.

As the kids got older and more cognitively engaging, their basic needs advanced also, and delegating became more challenging. My daughter was struggling with Latin grammar. My son gave me the stink-eye if I took business calls during his tennis matches. My youngest was avoiding going to the bathroom. Our wood floors flooded, quickly molded, and the whole downstairs had to be redone. And my husband's needs were relegated to a date-night-only status. Still, I proudly juggled all these daily twists and ignored the incremental fissures that were spreading into our supposedly perfect life. Sneaking away for work became increasingly tricky; however, I felt committed to being a serious, fully leaned-in professional. I slept less and doubled down on my work commitments.

Then, my closest brother got very sick, and it became clear he was not going to be cured. All else blurred, and I rearranged everything so I could spend his last months as close to him as possible. No longer was I chasing down the next spec script or coaxing a hot director to come aboard a movie. It became obvious that I increasingly cared less about the work. Instead, my priorities shifted to melanoma protocols, pain-management advocacy, and being honest about the inevitable, primal loss of my favorite brother. In the past, I was able to emotionally compartmentalize and remain a good worker and mother, but during that year of traveling and sitting beside my brother at various cancer hospitals across the country, I hit my breaking point, and I was crumbling.

Heartbreakingly, all the elite medicine and tireless endurance could not save my brother; he was only forty-four when we lost him peacefully at his home in Maine. A month later, I was fired from a job I should have been able to do in my sleep. For many months I blamed my new boss for firing me cruelly and unfairly, but the truth is that I had become a compromised worker. I was hovering in the slow lane in a business that did not make allowances for "flex" work hours. As I dug deeply and processed being fired, I had to ask myself: "If I had been my boss, what would I have done?" With a little perspective, I had to admit that I had drifted away from caring about my movie business job; my heart had a primal tear in it, and I had to go home and regroup.

Meanwhile, life kept me occupied. My daughter was running for ninth grade president and needed a behind-the-scenes campaign manager; my son played flag football six days a week and was always hungry for extra lunches and new cleats; and my youngest was mapping out an intricate trek up Mt. Everest by climbing every tree and fence in sight. Also, I miraculously had a fourth child, a change-of-life younger sister for my then-fifteen-year-old eldest daughter. It was time. They all deserved more mothering, so gradually but definitively, I became the stay-at-home parent. My days seemed busier than ever. I never found the time to read the trade papers or take a lunch meeting. Instead, I became absorbed by less definable, less lucrative, and less ego-gratifying tasks of managing a family charitable foundation, co-chairing a few school events, hosting a nonstop menagerie of kids and friends, and planning family adventures. My career paused and had become piecemeal—freelance projects, but nothing full-time or long-term. Somebody had to tend to the home front, and I won the job.

I was absolutely off the work highway. I shuddered when people asked, "What do you do?" I felt separate from some of my closest friends. As they were climbing up the corporate ladder, I was pinching strawberries at Thursday's farmers' markets with other moms. Once, I had been just as capable as my working girlfriends, but I lost my professional aura. I could not figure out how to bring meaningful work back into my life.

Reach-In Exercise: YOUR EXIT STORY.

Take this hour to write your exit story. Turn on your best break-up music and let 'er rip. Give a full, dramatic rendition of all the reasons you left your former work track, and all the people who you feel may have thwarted your professional happiness. Tell all, without judgment or editing. Write it. Dictate it. Draw it. Paint it. Sing it. This should be a stream-of-consciousness exercise. Then, when you're done, put it away. We'll pull it out in a few days, but until then, put it out of sight and out of mind.

Write it out:

- What happened?
- Did you make a conscious choice to fade out of your full-time career, or did it just happen half-consciously?
- Did you have a clean break, or did you turn against your own career to justify leaving it behind?
- What ball didn't find its way into your mitt?
- Did you *quit,* or were your *fired*? Doesn't really matter, you are not there anymore. But still, good to admit.
- Did you use stay-at-home parenting as an out for a career you grew tired of?
- Who let you down?
- What mistakes did you make?
- What missteps led you away from a satisfying career path?
- What nonwork opportunity was deeply fulfilling at the time, but maybe now isn't so fulfilling?
- What or whom did you resent? Your boss? Your family? Yourself?

Continued . . .

74

Your Exit Story:

_____

_____

_____

_____

_____

_____

_____

_____

_____

Now that you've got THAT out of the way . . . congratulations! You're letting go of the past so you can grab onto your future!

> ## Daily Do List
>
> ❑ Wrote (or painted or sang or danced) my exit story.
>
> ❑ Tucked away exit story in a safe place.
>
> ❑ Kept up with an organizational habit today. Cleaned one messy sector.
>
> ❑ Reached out to one Career Connection today . . . and logged it.

Hour Two
Write Your "Shoulda, Woulda, Coulda"

Now is your chance to play the blame game, just for a little while. Let's not get too crazy. Don't start calling past employers or going to old haunts and laying into people. Just allow a little time to get mad at someone or something that thwarted your career path . . . or, in the spirit of the exercise, an hour.

Think about everything that came up for you yesterday when you revisited the ghosts of your professional past. Most likely you feel some regret, and even resentment, targeted at someone specific. Give a name to your career nemesis. It could be an old boss who passed you up on your dream project, or your spouse, who asked you to quit your job to be with the kids, or the roadside AAA guy who was so late fixing your flat tire that you missed the meeting and lost the big client.

Or . . . *maybe* the exit-pusher was *you*. It's possible that the person you resent most in this whole stepping-off memory is yourself. That's okay. Today can be the day to do a little resentment exorcism, to beat up on that ick that's been stewing for a while now. Have at it.

There are always two sides to any separation. If you can, try to infuse your exit story with a few genuine pluses. Perhaps you never should have become a lawyer and never would have exited had you not been forced out. Perhaps you left your lucrative copy-writing job because your daughter was on her way to becoming a world-class gymnast. A fantastic path for your promising eight-year-old, but one that required you to become her full time advocate. Perhaps the time you spent care-taking your ailing dad was a priceless full circle that completed your father-daughter bonding. Plenty of times the stay-at-home decision was not only necessary but also the right choice and perhaps a cherished blessing. There is never a perfect choice. We can only do our best . . . And hindsight can be a cruel lens. You are here right now . . . No need to dwell on what might have been.

Just get it out and go!

How Did SHE Do It?
She took the high road, dug deep, and carried on.

Nina J., mother of three, film and TV producer and social activist, studio president

Nina was an excellent Studio President. And for eight years, as head of a motion picture studio, she was the guiding force of many hit movies and franchises including *The Sixth Sense*, *The Princess Diaries*, *Chronicles of Narnia*, and *Pirates of the Caribbean*.

Still, while she was in the delivery room with her wife, who was giving birth to their third child, Nina got a phone call from the studio chief that her contract was not going to be renewed. Publicly, Nina's release from her Presidency was deemed a "corporate restructuring," and quite quickly the male head of marketing was given her office. Although it was a shockingly crappy way to get fired, the sun still came up the next morning, and the world kept spinning. Nina was notoriously gracious and philosophic about her departure, stating that her work at the studio had been a "privilege, not an entitlement," and she knew that none of these rarefied jobs "last forever." Classy Lady.

Nina regrouped, discovered the value of her real friends, and soldiered on. No one could take away her talent or her dignity. Nina was definitely sad and bewildered and maybe a little scared, but she kept herself positive. Before you knew it, her "still Nina" producing and networking skills rebooted her career. Out of the fire, this phoenix has credits that include *The Hunger Games* and *The Wimpy Kids Franchises*, and most recently television's *The People v. OJ Simpson*.

It's been a happy outcome for Nina, her coping mettle was tested, and she rose to the occasion. She's never has forgotten the *value of getting fired as a growth opportunity*. Bravely, Nina sought out honest criticism from trusted friends. She faced the ugly truth as to why she had been rejected. Sure, Nina could have pointed plenty of fingers at others, but she knew her sweetest victory would come by righting her own ship. So she dug deep into her own culpabilities, mended a few holes, and carried on. For Nina, this "failure" opened the door to an alternate success. Of course her loss was intense and painful, but with time and persistence, her readjustments improved her as a person and as a producer.

Reach-In Exercise: WRITE YOUR REGRET LETTER.

Spend today writing a letter of regret to the person you think harmed you. Express your feelings and frustrations about what you feel went wrong, and why it was so-and-so's fault. If writing doesn't do it for you, think beyond the page: put your phone on airplane mode and "call" that person, take the dog for a walk in the woods, pretend you're in a real conversation, and explain your feelings.

Do whatever you need to vent, release, or express your bad feelings. Do it. Be dramatic. Don't hold back. But when you're truly done venting, let's be sure it's understood that you will *not* send that letter or make that phone call. No bridges will get burned here. Prudence is the watchword. All you're doing is simply releasing that gunky energy.

Liberate yourself from those feelings of victimhood. Smile. End your drama. Release the rubbish and make room for your reinvention.

And while we're on the subject of reinvention, feel free to take a minute to acknowledge the sparkly, silver lining in these past however-many years you've been home.

In fact, take a minute to be grateful for the goodies that came from your career exit.

Maybe they didn't all come at once, and maybe you have to dig deep to summon each memory now, but give it a whirl. Maybe exiting had a big, beautiful bunch of blessings.

It's quite possible you have no regrets. That's wonderful! Don't force yourself to scrounge up some loose regret between the sofa cushions. Nothing wrong with acknowledging the silver lining of your off-ramping and thanking the specific person or incident that incited your departure. Perhaps then you can use today's hour to travel down the avenue of gratitude toward whoever may have helped you through a tenuous career moment—or even someone who initially discouraged you but ultimately propelled you through and onto the other side of the road. Hindsight, and the perspective it offers, can be a wonderful thing.

However you spend this hour, make sure it's productive and transformative. Get real with yourself, acknowledge your stuff, and get over it by being accountable for the past. Your present and future self will thank you.

Daily Do List

❑ Wrote (or shouted) my regret letter to someone specific, without actually making the call or pressing "send."

❑ Released any negative feelings and moved on with my day.

❑ Continued with at least two organizational habits.

❑ Contacted by phone or email (and logged) at least one new support connection.

Hour Three
Never Walk Alone

Studies show that taking the scenic route to a career is costly and your financial intake suffers a 10 percent reduction per year for every year that you're off track. In other words, if you are removed from the workforce during the critical ages thirty-one to thirty-six, then you will be likely to lose 50 percent of your lifetime earning potential. In more instances than not, taking time off to raise a family didn't seem like an option. You were beckoned home. Whether you were summoned, or you were asked nicely, or you blissfully volunteered, the homeward shift seemed very necessary at the time. Now, if you want to return to the work force, you, too, can be part of bucking these statistics by picking the right job direction, emboldening yourself as a candidate, and *not giving up* on yourself.

Sylvia Ann Hewlett, President of the Center for Work-Life Policy at Harvard, reported, "While more than one-third (37%) of highly qualified woman off-ramp for some period of time, the vast majority (93%) want to return to work. Many find this more difficult than anticipated. Only 74% succeed in rejoining the workforce and only 40% return to full-time jobs. Those are the facts."

These numbers might not look great, but you're going to be the one to beat the odds. Plenty of other moms have walked away. Plenty have struggled to find good work, and they succeeded. You were not alone when you left work, and you will not be alone as you transition back. You, too, can succeed.

Potholes aside, if you really want to go for it, stick with this program, reach out to connections, and work at becoming a confident candidate. We are here to help with many of the to-dos and how-tos that lie ahead.

Reach-Out Exercise: SUMMON YOUR SUPPORT SYSTEM.

It's important to try to not go through this job hunt alone. With a little extra effort, you will discover that you are NOT alone. Today, ask your friends for their most embarrassing, harrowing, horrible, enraging exit and work stories. Also ask to hear their fondest professional memories, proudest accomplishments, most mortifying moments, and takeaway wisdom. Maybe invite the girls over for a "wine and dish" night—sit around and share your respective professional pasts (or presents)!

Work/life balance is a core issue for all moms. I have never met a mother who did NOT struggle with their mix of parenting/working/coupledom/singledom. It's a classic maternal tic to feel guilty about not being *good enough* and/or that there was a gross misstep on life's trajectory. Once asked, most women could spend hours dissecting their right-and-wrong turns, their regrets, and proud standouts.

A Conversation Starter Prompt

1. What was your answer when asked what you wanted to be when you grew up?:
   - As a Fifth Grader: _____
   - As a College Senior: _____
   - Right Now: _____
   What was the one thing you never did because you were embarrassed to say you wanted to do it?

2. Did you have an "Aha!" moment when you realized you could NOT do it all?
   - What quadrant of your life got most neglected?
     - Your kids or family, specifically your spouse.
     - Career advancement.
     - Community involvement or advocacy issues.
     - Your waistline or health.
     - Your moral compass or your dignity.
     - If you could have a do-over and redesign your work/life path, what would it look like?

3. Do you have friends who do NOT work?
   - Where do you meet them?
   - How do you intersect with them?
   - What tool do you use to keep your day organized?

4. As a Daughter, As a Mother:
   - How did your own mother pressure you in a particular work direction?
   - Do you remember a work-ethic mantra from YOUR mother?
   - Do you find yourself echoing a version of that mantra to YOUR daughters or sons?

5. What stands out as your proudest on-the-job moment?
   - . . . and your most mortifying?

If you are uncomfortable talking to contacts about their work path, I have attached a conversation starter (see previous page) that formed the basis of my interviews with women across the country. Most often, women became very engaged in musing about their path through life. It became an introspective release to let off the steam that comes from juggling twenty plates in the air every day.

As you delve, it's also fun to consider if there may be a girlfriend, sister, or even daughter who can answer these questions for you. Sometimes others can see you more clearly than you see yourself. This might be a former boss (if appropriate) or spouse/partner.

A Friendly Reminder: Stay On Top of Your Game.

Now that we have made it through week three of *Moms for Hire* boot camp, let's formalize your habits to keep organized.

- **Every** day, claim and schedule time to reclaim your autonomy and identity.
- **Every** night, check in with your to-do list.
- **Every** Wednesday, weed out one quadrant of your life.
- **Every** day, check and check off your to-do list.
- **Every** week, reach out to at least three new contacts.
- **Every** time you reach out to someone for something job-related, log it.

You've been pedaling along, building your organizational muscles. Now let's take off the training wheels.

Keep your Lists. Keep your Calendar. Keep your Organizing BFF happy.

DEB TELLS ALL

Just Keep Going . . . (a.k.a. Finding your Good Lie)
No matter how successful you are. Or how hard you work . . . how healthy or virtuous or careful you have been. Someday, a seismic tragedy will pass right over your neighbor's house and knock on your front door. The world is filled with random snowstorms, nasty viruses, and accidental car crashes, and that's before we happen upon wars, business flops, and divorces. So many turns can alter a family's structure forever. You cannot avoid all of life's twisted destinies. Inevitably at some point, we'll all draw a short straw. The way we cope with personal tragedy . . . how we fall apart, learn from our heartbreaks, and remend from aftermaths will become the blueprint for how we find our own "good lie."

Ten years ago, my forty-nine-year-old husband passed away without warning. It was devastating on every imaginable front. But as a mother of four, there was very little time to bask in the sadness. Someone had to set the tone for how we were going to carry on. With stoic resolve, I was going to shield my kids from a stigmatized fatherless life. They had one another and a fabulous extended family, and I had my loyal and ingenious girlfriends. Our whole village did our best to keep up that sense of fun and adventure that Bobby had always captained.

And while keeping his legacy alive was a wonderful intention, first I had to make a living. Shoes still needed buying and college tuitions still needed to be paid. I quickly had to dig deep into his files and see if there were any projects that could be monetized. I had no choice but to find his promising movie projects and turn them into viable currency.

Bobby had been in the movie business for his entire career, and he supported his family with some very fine films and some nicely commercial movies. The search of every bottom drawer was on . . . What could I uncover and push forward to keep this family housed and clothed?

One centerpiece script that Bobby had loved was based on a *60 Minutes* story about the Lost Boys of Sudan, called *The Good Lie*. It was a fictionalized dramatic retelling of the thousands of Sudanese Boys who had fled a horrible civil war that destroyed their village and country to survive as child refugees first in Africa and finally to America. Bobby loved these new Americans and their intense, impressive story. He spent countless hours listening and tirelessly advising many Lost Boys and Girls, hoping that some would become leading voices in their American diaspora. One particularly Lost Boy, Valentino Deng (who ended up being the subject of Dave Egger's book *What Is the What*), moved in with our family for several months, sharing a room with our twelve-year-old son while we all helped Valentino apply to a four-year college. Meanwhile, ever-passionate Bobby convinced a movie studio to develop a script, he found a very worthy director, and was in the process of pushing this film into production. And then, Bobby died.

It was up to me to carry this torch and to get this film produced. The script was fabulous, and the project was an asset that could not be wasted. I stepped in and did my best. But the budget had come in quite high. The director got busy with another movie. The movie studio's interest waned. Other financing dried up, and the project seemed lost without Bobby at the helm. Of course, I was quite saddened that I could not push this project to a greenlight; I had many other uphill battles to wage.

Meanwhile, my family and I remained quite supportive and involved with many of the Lost Boys and their adjustment to America. I helped several Lost Boys and Girls get into colleges and business schools. We formed a national network for the groups of refugees scattered in Phoenix, Atlanta, Jacksonville, Syracuse, San Jose, etc. We found grants to sponsor a few Lost Boy conferences across the country. We developed a cohesive website. And we created a Mission trip to Sudan for the Boys to reunite with their families they had not seen in decades.

Yes, I failed at getting this very very difficult movie produced, but my caring never stopped. My whole family stayed engaged in humanitarian causes of South Sudan, and to this day, many of the five thousand American Lost Boys and Girls still insist on calling me "Mama Deb."

Daily Do List

❑ Reached out to friends for their positive and negative work memories.

❑ Added to my Contacts and Connections list.

❑ Proactively organized a bonding-and-dish night with like-minded souls.

❑ Remembered that I am not alone. Others have experienced unemployment trauma, and they've made it through.

❑ Purged my bookshelves and neatened my *Mom for Hire* space.

Hour Four
Give Value to Your Misty Watercolor Memories

To all of you in the thick of wiping little noses, cramming for a photosynthesis test, or making a late night run to Target for a soccer mouthguard, your working life seems like a million years ago. In other ways, you feel like it was just yesterday. Today, we're going to relive your workdays, and we can refine what *kind* of job you could best pursue.

Reach-In Exercise: LIST THE DELIGHTS AND HORRORS OF YOUR FORMER WORK LIFE.

Make a list of everything you loved and everything you detested about your old job(s) or career(s). Be specific, be general . . . whatever it takes to write out whatever comes into your head. No judgments; just spew. Here are my examples, which might inspire your streaming process:

Work Perks (My Sweet List):

- Pregame caffeine at the local coffee shop. That first sip of a double capp.
- Staff meetings I was prepped for.
- Meetings with smart, talented people.
- Running into unexpected people in the hallway.
- Finishing a difficult task. Pressing "send."
- The 4 o'clock cookie break and interoffice flirt.
- Scouting and hiring new writers, directors, executive team members.
- Mentoring and then delegating to emerging and deserving associates.
- Reading the entertainment trades and *being* in the trades.
- Going to the set of a movie I had developed.
- Researching any subject (dinosaurs, South Sudan, college pranks, etc.) and still calling that *work*.
- My office—itself another place to go.
- The paycheck. The expense account. Money.
- Pitching my idea to someone smarter than yours truly; getting positive feedback.
- Having good health insurance for my whole family.

Continued . . .

- Spirited office camaraderie.
- Having job security.

Your Sweetest Triumphs:

- _____
- _____
- _____

My Sour List:

- Fear of being a fraud/lacking self-confidence.
- Dealing with powerful people who might think I'm not good enough.
- Having to tell someone they were not "good enough."
- Hiring someone who might get me fired.
- Fear of being rejected.
- Actually being rejected.
- Losing my creative mojo (a.k.a. executive block).
- Getting yelled at because my boss was mad at something else.
- And in turn, yelling at someone because I was frustrated by something else.
- Missing out on a book or script I should have scouted and found.
- Missing out on a parenting moment because I was away or distracted.
- Reading a script or seeing a movie that I pushed for turn out worse than expected.
- Reading a bad review of my project that I kind of agreed with.
- Not sleeping enough.
- Not having control of my schedule.
- Pressure, stress, excessive competition.
- Shoulda, woulda, coulda—replaying a bad scene over and over. Beating myself up for not having a better comeback.
- Constantly second-guessing myself.

Your Job Torments:

- _____
- _____
- _____

Continued . . .

Professional Skills I Was/Am Most Proud Of:

- Working harder than anyone else in the office.
- Being diligent and tenacious. Never giving up on an idea.
- Writing a smart argument . . . that worked convincingly.
- Being well liked in the office.
- Being the go-to answer girl regarding the next big talent.
- Being trusted by and loyal to a boss.
- Being head of a team.
- Mastering a task quickly; being a fast learner.
- Embracing change and new technology.
- Never minded getting hands dirty.
- Good at delivering bad news and firing people.

Professional Skills You Are/Were Most Proud of:

- _____
- _____
- _____

These skill lists will become particularly important when you identify your transferable skills later on in these steps. For now, grab a highlighter and circle the moments and feelings you want to *keep and nurture*. Then take a different color highlighter and cross out the feelings you want to *discard*. Even if you switch careers and pursue a new field, many of your skills are transferable like that classic black dress of the professional days—versatile and trusty.

Categorize Your Happiest Role

Success is always easier when you're doing something you love, but it's maybe difficult to admit you own ambition. Before you start actively looking for jobs, you must identify the borders of your comfort zone.

Once you can define what "happy work" means to you, you can excel and spread your wings within your best boundaries, without always having to play it safe. With a thoughtful sense of what makes you thrive, guess what? You *will* thrive because you will exude confidence, self-esteem, and be a highly sought-after candidate.

Imagine the Super Bowl is coming up, and there's going to be a party. What role do you take on? Do you offer to host? Do you bring the football-themed appetizers? Do you only want to watch the game? Or are you only coming for the half-time commercials and socializing? Would you rather be the kid wrangler and hang out with them, playing Twister? Do you take charge of the betting grid and handle the cash? Are you the one collecting the half-empty Solo cups and folding the throw blankets? Does the idea of a party totally overwhelm you—you'd rather watch the game at home?

Imagine what role you'd be most excited by taking on (or what roles seem easiest for you to accomplish). Now, think of a similar situation in recent memory—a PTA meeting, benefit, house-painting project, joint birthday party for one of your kids, neighborhood festival, or town meeting.

- What piece of the project did you contribute?
- What job actually seems awesome, but intimidating?
- What job do you always avoid?
- Did you volunteer for a task, or were you assigned one?

Identify the characteristics of each role that feel safe and comfortable to you. Try to delineate your particular skillset and your comfort zone now.

Reach-In Exercise: WHAT KIND OF WORKER ARE YOU?

Once you get involved in a project, what role do you take on? What role do you step into at a school committee function or church event, your child's birthday party, or dealing with a newly broken bathtub? Imagine you are a parent of a sixth grader, and all the parents are creating a tribute to the graduation class. In the past, parents have produced a song, a book, a video that they reveal to the entire class at graduation. What role do you assume in this project?

Assign a number from 1 to 5 in the questionnaire on the next page, as to how you see yourself participating in this project, with "1" indicating you avoid that task or feel the *least* qualified, and "5" meaning you enjoy that piece of the project and consider yourself *super* qualified.

Continued . . .

Are you a(n) . . .

- Initiator/Creator: You THINK UP the project?   _____
- Administrator/Servicer: You ORGANIZE the project?   _____
- Worker Bee/Facilitator: You IMPLEMENT the project?   _____
- Salesman/Marketer: You SELL the project?   _____
- Detail Finesser/Sweeper: You FINISH the project?   _____
- Caterer/Facilities Manager: You ENSURE food & health?   _____
- Cheerleader/Enthusiasm Coach: You SUPPORT the project?   _____
- Observer: You WATCH and WITNESS the project?   _____

Clarify and Circle Your True North

- Do you get more pleasure from cooking up the concept or from being assigned a task?
- Do you work better with your head or your hands?
- Do you prefer to work alone or in a group?
- Do you want to have a boss or be the boss?
- Are you willing to invest some savings in starting up a business?
- Can you travel with your job, or do you need to be home for dinner/bedtime?
- How important is location to you? Distance from home? Schools?
- Is it best for you to work night hours or early morning?
- Which kid-shift can you share with spouse or helper—morning or evening?
- Can you work a forty-hour week or is twenty-five hours a week your limit?
- Do you need to work at a company that offers family medical benefits?
- Do you want to work as an entrepreneur or in a corporate structure?
- How important is size of the company? Do you prefer a corporate or boutique office setting?
- Are you drawn to non-profit or for-profit?
- Does your dream job require further educational degrees?
- Do you want to dress up for work or do you want a jeans and t-shirt job?
- What is the paycheck you need to bring home in order to compensate for your leaving home?

Continued . . .

For sure, these are not the only questions that matter. But along with fantasizing, you also need to think about how your job passions can align with your domestic realities. Once you have answered these questions, let's prioritize them even further. If you have any other parameters and obstacles that are crucial to your job hunt, list and take notice of them now.

_____

_____

_____

_____

_____

Finally, if you haven't yet taken this astoundingly perceptive Personality Test—www.16personalities.com—instead of rechecking your Instagram or playing another round of Candy Crush, set aside ten minutes to answer these easy questions. It will help you sharpen your "who am I" knife and make you a more pointed and effective job seeker.

Daily Do List

☐ Reminisced about the delights and horrors of my former work life.

☐ Identified the roles I'm comfortable in, which helped me define the boundaries of my comfort zone.

☐ Kept up with two organizational habits: one personal, one desktop.

☐ Reached out to a new connection; followed up on Connection Log.

Hour Five

Clean Your Slate . . . Discover the Next You

> *"Whatever happens to you belongs to you. Make it yours.*
> *Feed it to yourself even if it feels impossible to swallow.*
> *Let it nurture you, because it will."*
> —Cheryl Strayed, *Dear Sugar*

The Brazilians throw flowers and rings into the ocean to please the gods at the start of each year. The Jews throw stale bread into the water at the end of their new year to rid themselves of disappointments from the past. The Catholics light candles; the Yogis (and modern-day spiritualists) burn sage. All of these are physical manifestations of a process of closure. And all feel good. Today, let's create a ritual to say good-bye to the regret and loss you've been associating with your old career.

Reach-In and Reach-Out: BYE-BYE BAD STUFF.

The moment of truth: take out your exit story and your voodoo letter. Read it as though you were watching the movie of someone else's life. How did you portray yourself? Hero-ically? A noble woman sacrificing her ego and self for the sake of her family's well-being? As a victim? Sabotaged by a terrible boss or coworker, cut down in the prime of her career? Or were you simply at a crossroads? It's likely that there's a bit of truth In each of these characterizations. There's also probably an equal bit of delusion, too. We're all really good at repainting a narrative to make the events fit our emotional memory of them. But what's past is past, and now it's time to let go.

From here on out, notice when you play the victim card and stop yourself. It's a dangerous, unattractive place to be, and it will never help you. Do whatever you can to muscle your way out of the victimized state of mind and watch how your life starts to change. Today, take control of your story. You don't yet know what the ending will be, but *you* are the one writing it. Begin today by deflating the energy of your past regrets, resentments, blames, shames, and setbacks, and transform it into future work mojo.

Continued . . .

Take out your regret letter and burn it (safely)! You don't have to do this alone, either. Make a s'mores night with the kids and indulgently chuck it in the fire pit. Feel all that stagnant emotion move out of you. Make room for a clean slate, a few more hours in the day . . . and a path forward.

. . . And good riddance!

Take a breath. This week you have delved into past professional pains. You've given your psychological roadblocks a name (person, organization, fate, etc.), and now you can push past these obstacles. You have spent much of this week cleansing *intellectually* and *emotionally*, and today you can take pleasure in cleaning out some aspects of your *physical* life.

Clean 'er out reminder. What portion of your clutter did you purge this Wednesday?

There is no magic potion to make you keep your house, your car, your computer, and your mind organized. *Being neat* and *completing tasks* are healthy habits. And habits need to be repeated and repeated to create muscle memories. We all know life is more productive when you inhabit an organized zone. I have offered helpful hints, but you need to find your own pleasure in being tidy. And then, you need to repeat and repeat those habits—perhaps with a bit of obsession—until they stick.

Daily Do List

❑ Reread my exit story and regret letter. Disposed of them.

❑ Transmuted the physical manifestation of my negative past into motivational energy for the future. Burn, baby . . . burn!

❑ Cleaned out at least one closet.

❑ Shifted my mindset to a clean-slate zone.

❑ Looked ahead, not down.

Step Four

MOTHERHOOD'S MADE
YOU BETTER.

Nicely done. By now you have completed the first three steps of *Mom for Hire*. Let's take stock of your accomplishments: You've claimed some personal space and time. You've told your people that you are ready. You've become more organized in your thoughts and actions. You've voiced your psychological hold-ups and relegated them to your past. The move is on; now let's enjoy this fourth step as you launch into being an irresistible *Mom for Hire*.

The promise of this fun week is to boost your confidence and free up some extra time for job-hunting. You'll start by validating those perfect "mom moments" and reminding yourself how motherhood actually made you better—a more ingenious, more efficient, and more flexible worker. Then, you'll home in on the nitty-gritty of job search prep so you're ready to go out and get that job!

Hour Goals

Hour One:	**Write** your *Mom Résumé*.
Hour Two:	**Deputize** kids and partner to specific commissions.
Hour Three:	**Evaluate** your "launch-ability."
Hour Four:	**Update** your social media profiles.
Hour Five:	**Find** the voice "To Ask."

Hour One
Find Your Mom Value

"Mothering is the only job you can never quit."
—Tina Fey, *Bossypants*

This job is a permanent gig; you are a parent for life. That child is never going back into the toothpaste tube. So, as long as you are always going to be a mother, you might as well enjoy the perks of parenting!

Over a decade ago, award-winning journalist Anne Crittenden wrote *If You've Raised Kids, You Can Manage Anything: Leadership Begins at Home*. Her well-researched premise is that the very "Mom skills" you perfect in your everyday routines are readily transferable to leadership powers at the office.

Everyday, Mom's leadership skills are tested. She has had to become an on-the-job expert in:

- Communicating with employees.
- Resolving employee disputes.
- Handling company finances and making strategic budget cuts.
- Teaching ethics and values as an everyday code.

For me, after plenty of great career experiences and some legit résumé successes, I often feel like "a lucky fraud" (even now!). Chalk it up to insecurity. Honestly, though, I have not always been gainfully employed, and even when I had an impressive job, it always seemed there was someone doing better than me. So whenever I am asked those four dreaded words, "What do you do?" I can still seize up and stutter. It can even be more jolting when I run into an ex-colleague who, trying to avoid the what-do-you-do question, instead asks, "How are the kids doing?"

Even if this wasn't the intent, these simple questions too often feel loaded, diminishing, and can trigger a paralyzing defense. Thus, many nonworking moms end up hibernating or gravitating away from the working mom groups. And the *Mommy War* divide emerges. Of course, those who ask are just trying to make polite conversation, but face it: they're damned if they ask about my empty job status, and they're insulting if they *only* ask about the kids.

Instead of avoiding other working moms or dads, go to that dinner party prepared for that awkward question. Along with the house gift, come armed with a back-pocket of humorous retorts. My favorite quip was from the hilarious actress and author Alexandra Wentworth, who could proudly answer, "I created human life . . ." So, I started asking others. Here's a few hashtag-able tips to proudly validate wherever your "mom-ness" has taken you.

When Asked: "What Are You Doing Now?"

- Living vicariously through my children.
- Plotting my un-retirement.
- If you've seen my pool man, you wouldn't go to work, either.
- Writing a blog called *The Bitch is in the House.*
- Producing perfect children.
- Wrecking my otherwise perfect children.
- Turning into my mother.
- Rebelling against my mother.
- Getting my master's in cooking, chauffeuring, and collecting.
- Planning my daughter's Bat Mitzvah. *But I thought your daughter is three?* Yep!

At one of these unnerving moments, I step back, focus on my own mental health, and let go of all my self-judgments. I find the kernel of validation in my day that makes me feel good and strong. It wasn't all bad . . . you'll get through it if you look for your win instead of your losses. Let that positive nugget become a warming mantra. Repeat it whenever you feel stinky. Balance will follow.

- "I'm doing my best and that IS my job."
- "The kids are thriving . . . and today, most of their dirty socks found their way to the hamper."
- "Although the dryer's on the fritz and we missed the school bus, my teenager agrees that my classic playlist is brilliant!
- "My career is still in a stall, but that chicken dish I just invented knocked it out of the park."
- "I had a great run on the beach."
- "I checked off another Step en route to becoming a *Mom For Hire.*"

Find your victories. And let them sustain you through your day.

We have been bombarded with statistics for off-ramped moms struggling to get back to rewarding employment. Plan on being an exception to whatever the statistics are forboding; it's important to remember that you are not alone. The quest to *have it all* is an age-old challenge for all active moms . . . and what does it mean, really? That tricky balance of career and family happiness is an ever-swinging pendulum.

The only way through the *having it all* debate is to stop looking at other people's green lawns. Stay centered and find personal pleasure where you are *right now*. By doing that, you will gain courage and momentum to change things if they're out of whack. If you think you're not enjoying mothering, you may want to think again; the only way to enjoy life is to cherish your *own* happy gene. No matter how great motherhood *or* a job is or isn't. Only you can control your own mental health.

So, What Happened to Your Paycheck?

While you may have been off-the-working-grid for some time, I guarantee you have not been idle. The following chart reflects the monetary value of stay-at-home laborers.

What Is a Stay-At-Home Mom Worth?

On average, stay-at-home moms juggle 96.5 hours of work each week.[3]

- Facilities manager: 10.9 hours at $31.68
- CEO: 3.2 hours at $53.81
- Laundry operator: 6.5 hours at $10.10
- Computer operator: 8.6 hours at $16.44
- Housekeeper: 14.6 hours at $10.19

- Cook: 14.5 hours at $14.04
- Day care teacher: 14.3 hours at $12.84
- Van driver: 7.8 hours at $10.14
- Psychologist: 8.3 hours at $38.94

Whenever I need a boost, I refresh my bruised ego with a *Forbes* magazine article that computes all the services moms provide without pay to our children and our home. Bottom line, if moms were to get paid the going rate for driving, tutoring, travel-agenting, cooking, etc., they would earn $118,000 a year.

---

[3]Facts and figures from salary.com

96

At one point, I drew up a mock résumé of the various labor experience and talents I've accumulated while mothering four children, running a household, and being a mate and "coparenter." For me, creating a "mom résumé" gave my hours/days/months/years great validation. Every mom job hunter can take a peek at my "Jane Mom" résumé and perhaps, nodding her head, remind herself she is doing plenty of great work.

Chances are, this isn't your first mom rodeo. Sure, each child comes with unique challenges (special talents, special needs, special patience-testing stages). Sure, there will always be child-rearing setbacks (an offending tooth, an insurmountable bully, a frustrated test taker). But after a few years of being a mother, you've gotten better at the household tasks, you've mastered daily routines, and you've gotten ahead of your little rascals' tricks.

Hopefully, by now, "You've Got This." You've outsmarted some of your kid's quirks and uncovered short cuts into your family's habits. Soon, you will hit your 10,000-hour mark and become a mom expert (many of you already have). In most cases, by the time you are ready to press that I-want-more button, you've become a seasoned pro at parenting and all things home. Just be careful not to throw the baby out with the bathwater, especially if that fresh talcum smell is one of your most cherished memories.

Although this mom résumé is specific to my personal task list, I would bet that at least half of these services also fall within your day. For me, it was very validating to list my daily details down on paper, as it justified many of what I believed to be idle hours. Turns out, I didn't just *feel* busy; I *was* busy.

Jane Mom Resume   Hidden Valley, USA
Work Experience: Four Kids, One Dog, and One Backyard Vegetable Garden

Child Psychologist   Discipline and ego booster/four kids daily   ($100 per hour)
Chauffeur/Traffic Negotiator 15,000 miles a year of kid deliveries   ($20 per hour)
Restaurateur   Shop, plan, cook, and serve twenty meals a week for average of 8 people (Minimum wage + tips)
Travel Agent   Design and implement three family holiday trips per year   ($20 per hour)
Host/Party Planner   Four home events a month/two city-wide benefits per year   ($40 per hour)
Librarian   Re-read every classic book for Pre-K to 12th   ($25 per hour)
Sports Manager   Coach, team-mom, cheerleader, fan   ($15 per hour)
Nurse/Pharmacist   Predict child's temperature without a thermometer   ($30 per hour)
Frontline Contractor   Leak, computer, appliance, sewer Line, IT & DVR Expert   ($40 per hour)
Closet Organizer/
   Interior Designer   From sock-drawers to dining room.   ($25 per hour)
Family Archivist   Twenty years of family photos scanned and organized.   ($25 per hour)
Tutor   Homework project manager, SAT prompter, college counselor   ($75 per hour)

Volunteer   *Trustee of Family Charitable Foundation   (Some Expense)
                            *Mentor at-risk teenager with college-bound potential
                            *Neighborhood Board of Directors—Halloween & Mitzvah Committee

School Activist   *Career Day Chair at daughter's High School (five hours a week)
                            *Tour Ambassador at son's Middle School (two hours a week)
                            *Room Mom—1 year per kid in Elementary School (one hour a week)
                            *Organize School Walk-a-thon at Pre-school (twenty-five hours to complete)

Education

Parenting 101 (At bookstores/kids' schools/carpool lanes)

- Twenty years cumulative weekly trips to Barnes and Noble/Amazon Books/Internet Surfing
- Eight years cumulative Mommy-and-Me classes
- Decades of other moms' & siblings' tips and criticisms

Literary Scholarship Seminars (at home and in cars)

- Two book clubs per month
- 10,000 miles per year of audio books

Masters in Home Management (MHM)

- Field trips to four different food markets per week
- Constant comparative shopping for "same product that just costs less"
- Negotiating with plumber, carpet cleaner, handyman, et al.
- Light bulb, computer, telephone, cable and Wifi professional

Other Interests

- Bachelor of Fine Arts
- 2½ foreign languages
- Being sporty
- Eighteen Years Film Executive & Producer
- Finding a new husband
- Not looking tired

Mom Awards

- Stairmaster Record Holder: Basement Gym
- Brentwood School: Mother of the Year Award '07 and '11
- Family Champion: Jeopardy
- Executive Member at Costco

Reach-In Excercise: WRITE YOUR MOM RÉSUMÉ.

Now it's your turn. Proudly, lovingly, and with a sense of humor, write your mom résumé. List anything you could possibly be compensated for and give it a monetary value. Also, just for yourself, give it a *mom* value; there is worth beyond financial measure in all you have done for your family. Don't discount that.

YOUR NAME

HOURS: VALUE:

Mom Jobs:

❖
❖
❖
❖
❖

Mom Education:

❖
❖
❖

Non-Mom Interests:

❖
❖
❖
❖
❖

Mom Awards & Ambitions :

❖
❖
❖
❖
❖

If you are too busy or too tired to compose your own mom résumé, just grab a pen and circle the Jane Mom's tasks you, too, complete every day. Reach into the routines of your day, and find pleasure in those accomplishments. Allow yourself a silver lining realization that motherhood made you better. Not only did mothering give you a new perspective on the world, it also gave you plenty of under-the-radar skills that your MBA and RN degrees never covered.

So let yourself swagger a bit. Take a moment to rest on the laurels of a leadership talent that you were pushing forth every mom day. Be generous with yourself. This step is meant to convince you that even your average routines are often unexamined heroics. Don't forget that day in and day out you deal with some very difficult people in very difficult situations.

> *"Allow yourself to experience 'perfect moments.'*
> *The days are long, but the years are short."*
> —Gretchen Rubin, *The Happiness Project*

Today, let's dedicate some time to recognizing your stay-at-home happy time. For me, daytime bonus moments include that 8:15 post-drop-off second cup of coffee in a quiet house, gardening in the daylight, an occasional noon yoga class, being a tour guide at my son's middle school, watching my daughter master her first axel, a spontaneous lunch date with a friend.

And being appreciative of *yourself* is a muscle that needs regular workouts. Within the mom psychology of your busy, caring-for-others day, it's easy to just keep moving and not stop to acknowledge the delights of our sunny moments.

Dial Down Your Inner Debbie Downer

The older I get, the wiser my mother becomes. Her steadfast rule was that she could never buy a single new piece of clothing without giving away or clearing out an equivalent item from her closet. Likewise, my mom demanded that for every time I hated on something or complained about a person, I also had to state a random compliment to the world. However true my criticism might be, the negative words were never allowed to linger on as the last word.

Sadly, I have taken more morning hikes and sat through many lunchtime book clubs where wives stream off complaint-after-complaint about their working and unappreciative spouse.

- Can you believe my spouse won't let me redo the kitchen?
- My spouse is so tough on the kids . . . he should try being with them all day!
- I can never get my partner to help around the house.
- My partner belittles me for not going back to work, yet thinks the house will fall apart if I do go back.
- My spouse is always gone, and I don't have a minute to myself.

While *Moms for Hire* does not focus on marital relationships, please, please do not let your less-than-supportive mate be the excuse for you not finding satisfying work. Either accept your marriage or don't, but stop complaining; it's a waste of energy, and everyone is tired of hearing about it. Trust me.

Instead, if you pay close attention, every day you will witness glorious moments of delight that are sitting right in front of you. Pay attention to the unnoticed joy in your life. Let the good stuff in. I don't mean the obvious stuff, like the day your son got into college or when your daughter performed Chopin at the recital. I mean the little moments, seconds, inches, and feet that make up your day. It's often the less flashy, more character-driven moments that need appreciation. Look for them.

Shout-Out Your Perfect Moments.

Frequently, and out-of-the-blue, I can be heard declaring, "I am having a perfect moment!" And often those within earshot look around quizzically wondering what miraculous comet they might have missed. It's usually not much of a sight. It's rarely my son's soccer goal; instead it's the moment when he ties his own cleats. These perfect moments can be glances, conversations, car rides, or entire chunks of the day. Here are others to help get your gratitude muscle flexing:

- We are all sitting around a cramped dinner table, picking off one another's plate, laughing and talking, poking insider fun at one another.
- My son is away at college, but we are listening to his Spotify playlist he left behind for us.
- My girlfriends and I all sneak away for a night of gossip and giggles.
- My husband sends me flowers and signs the card "a secret admirer."

- A busy friend rearranges her day to pick me up from the airport because we needed a catch-up.
- Overhearing my eleven-year-old talk to the dog about her bad day at school.
- Looking at the photos of my disabled sister getting to swim with dolphins.

These are communal moments when everyone contributes to our family's connection. It's usually not a planned moment, but an intersecting slice of all our own lives; we just *are*. It's love.

Think back over the last week, and **list five perfect moments.**

1. _____
2. _____
3. _____
4. _____
5. _____

Now, think back over the last week, and list five things you got to do because you are NOT working. (For example, Tuesday tennis match, Wednesday fourth-grade field trip to the Endeavor Space Ship. Had the extra 40 minutes to steam-clean the kid-stained car seats.)

1. _____
2. _____
3. _____
4. _____
5. _____

A fun dinner table ritual many families put into their routine is called *The Rose and The Thorn*. Before dessert, each family member gets to announce the best and the worst thing that happened to them that day. So easy and such a good habit (e.g. my rose: the new drought resistant–grass lawn is still green; my thorn: losing my glasses . . . again).

Another way to make sure you appreciate something each day is to tie it into your daily to-do list. Before listing your intentions for the day, add three things you are grateful for or simply three things that give you pleasure.

Daily Do List

- ❏ Assigned a proud value to my transferable skills.

- ❏ Wrote (or adapted) my Mom Résumé.

- ❏ Witnessed and announced perfect moment(s).

- ❏ Swept up one still-messy quadrant of my house/car/desktop.

- ❏ Started my day, compiling a to-do list.

- ❏ Ended my day, checking off the list.

Hour Two
Delegate Your Mom Overload

This exercise can be tricky because it requires a psychological shift in the way you've positioned your "momself" within your family dynamic. It's common for a mother to be the selfless giver. Traditionally, the "good mom" is self-sacrificing to a fault—if she allows it to be that way.

It's important to feel like you're not the only one making the family world go 'round, and that every family member becomes active in the home. One way to encourage this is to institute a family plan that shares household jobs.

Reach In Exercise: LIST YOUR DAILY MOM DEEDS.

Today, grab a sturdy piece of paper and a pen. List the minutiae of your daily mom tasks. What did you do today for the house, garden, kids, and spouse? Compute your "don't worry, I'll do it" duties. Now add up all the things you say "yes" to.

Mom's Daily Feats:

- _____

- _____

- _____

And then today, you are going to look at that blasted list and simply say "no" to some of those items. Victory for mom!

Of course there are pieces of your stay-at-home job you can delegate. If you get pushback from your spoiled housemates, you can tie it to an allowance or dessert quota. Even if each giveaway task only amounts to a five-minute job, those five minutes of relief (e.g., taking out the garbage bags or making the bed) add up, and miraculously you'll quickly accrue a usable chunk of mom time.

With a bit of family retraining, there will come a point when you will never have to set a table again, nor will you carry down your daughter's hampered laundry. And guess what. They might even enjoy making their own smoothies (and clean up after).

Everyone wins here. The mom gets a break, and the kids learn about efficiency, responsibility, and teamwork, three hugely important traits to carry with them down their own life roads. Not to mention, when they get to college, they will know how to use the washing machine and cook a meal. Family accountability matters. Ask yourself and ask your kids, if they don't put their books back on the shelf, "who do they think will?" As a mom, your doing it all for the household does everyone a huge disservice. Begin delegating.

No longer will you need to feel that everyone "just watches while I do the mopping." Begin re-assigning. And before you even get a new job claim that your time has value—if you need to, post that Forbes magazine article on the family fridge right next to the list of new assignments. Refresh your spirit and remember that your time is worth a lot of money.

Change the narrative. Mom doesn't need to do everything—we're all self-sufficient. I'm not suggesting you tell your five-year-old he can walk home from school, or assign the seven-year-old to babysit the toddler, but kids are way more capable than many people (including many parents!) give them credit for. They want to participate. It helps give them a sense of value. From a very early age, they can learn to help out around the house and be more independent. Begin freeing up your minutes by giving generously of your tasks. Start today.

Involve the Kids.

Stop with the "selfless" caretaking . . . and never call them *chores*; instead, rename them *fun activities*. Start with the classic Tom Sawyer whitewashing trick and try convincing your impressionable offspring that these jobs are fun. If that doesn't work, bribe them with stars and stickers (you'll find my daughter Billi's chart on page 110). The sooner you start down the road of instilling family helping habits, the better. You will be surprised at how capable the little ones are in running the household and running themselves. Even when kids appear lazy, they actually have more energy than any of us parents!

And always, always have your kids come with you on errands—the dry cleaner, the car wash, the market, the frame store. You don't need to figure out a way for them to be at home while you're running around picking up oranges and snacks for their soccer game. Never apologize to your kids for wasting their time. Bring them with you and let them see how the work of your day happens. And while you're at it, have them load the groceries into the car. Let them run into the pharmacy to fetch the antibiotics. Give them the honor of pumping the gas and cleaning the windshield.

Let me be very clear about something before you get started on delegating: You might not like the way they do things. There could be streak marks on your windshield that drive you

105

bananas. Maybe they don't load the dishwasher with all of the plates facing the same way. Their sheets might not be tucked into the corners like a five-star hotel. And they might not know how to set a table using precise Emily Post guidelines, but they get the job done the best they can. Never again tell yourself it is easier to "just do it yourself." Leave it alone—don't get micromanagerial and start futzing with the job they did. It devalues their effort, and perfectionism is unattractive. Stop it. Life as you know it *will* go on quite well even if the napkins aren't folded in a perfect right angle.

"Every mom needs a wife."
—Amy Poelher

Reach-Out Exercise: MOM GIVEAWAYS.

Today, let's find a way to get your kids to contribute to the maintenance and the personality of their home. If you do all the work and navigate the household, those kids will always feel entitled, and you will always be at-their-service.

Here are a few guidelines to help you harness their energy . . . and hand over a few of the age-appropriate tasks they are capable of carrying out. So many of these tasks might feel minuscule and frankly are often easier to do yourself. However, all those five-minute tasks add up . . . and before you know it, you have accumulated an extra hour to do something that gives you pleasure. Also, all these giveaway tasks will create more capable children.

However, please note that:

- Every family is different: These are MY wishful markers, and honestly, I fail at many of these benchmarks often.
- This is just a guide; create your own family-specific *Giveaway List*.
- If they drop it, they pick it up. If they play with it, they put it away. Most important is accountability.
- For fun, hang this *Giveaway List* up somewhere public near the fridge or the snack drawer—and see how the crowd reacts.
- And, as always, just do your best.

Age Markers

AGE 2–3
- Schlep with you on family errands.
- Make eye-contact, say "hello" and "thank you."
- Begin a "clean floor" policy.
- 2 points for every item dunked into hamper, 3 points for everything dunked in the trash.

AGE 4–6
- Help set table and clear dishes.
- Put garbage in trash (recycle vs. trash vs. compost).
- Sweep floor.
- Sort silverware.
- Brush teeth, wash-up and self-bathe.
- Pickup toys . . . put away projects.
- Carry inside and unpack groceries.
- Take ownership and care of pet.
- Pack backpack for school.

AGE 7–10
- Set the table for dinner and clear the table.
- Load and unload the dishwasher.
- Take out the trash (blue vs. brown vs. green bin.)
- Help cook and clean a family dinner for one meal a week.
- Make their own school lunches.

AGE 11–12
- Do their own homework and assignments.
- Add their schedule to family calendar.
- Organize their own sporting equipment and packs.
- Look after younger siblings while mom chills.
- Keep their own calendar, set their own morning alarm.
- Write their own thank you notes.

TEENAGERS
- Fully responsible for room and stuff.
- Can babysit and think about afterschool job.
- Mow lawn and shovel snow.
- Plan a family adventure.

Delegating Means Dad, Too.

Even beyond the obvious praise of family dinners as the crucial, plus centerpiece of a healthy home life, there is plenty of data proving that family dinners help kids become smarter, healthier, happier, more accomplished, and less troubled teens and adults.

For a consistently-eating-dinner-together plan to work, it is important that the working mate is included in these family scenes. This may require some insistence on the part of the stay-at-home partner.

In fact, with most of the long-haul successful marriages I have witnessed, the working spouse often takes control of creating either dinner or family breakfast for the household.

It's up to you to not let the paycheck-receiving dad become self-righteous. Instead, he needs to help set an example for an active, home-life participant.

How Did SHE Do It?
She insisted her marriage become a real partnership.

Abigail J., coparent of three, copartner at Internet company, Redwood City, California

Abigail met her husband Andrew in her late twenties when she was a rising political strategist in Washington, DC. He had just founded a savvy tech start-up, and was exactly Abby's kind of adorable. They fell in love, and his career skyrocketed. Although they were both East Coasters, the silicon industry pulled them West. The couple moved to California and began a new adventure as husband and wife and, quickly, as parents. The new coast, new babies, and a new culture was a shock to Abby, and as her husband's career whizzed upward, her career derailed. She kept herself gracefully busy with three small children, their active home, and rebuilding her political and nonprofit networks in California. And she was always proud of her husband's successes. She was wistful about her abandoned career and refinding her own professional calling felt like moonlighting on the night shift. Never enough time and energy. And, like so many wives of megamen, her career shifted to new mega-Viking stove's back burner.

Yet in her own backyard, parenting had to be equalized. Quite emphatically: "If we are going to remain a family, we both have to be in it." Andrew was not given the option to be a halfway father. He had to figure out a way to actively co-parent. So he rallied himself every morning to share family breakfast launch and drive the

Continued . . .

---

http://www.casacolumbia.org/addiction-research/reports/importance-of-family-dinners-2012
http://thefamilydinnerproject.org/resources/faq/

kids to school. After drop-off, he could be Mr. Start-up all day long—and often late into the night. Dad caught on quickly and only occasionally had to be reminded that his career-as-a-Dad was—at least—equal to any other job on his plate. Although he might grumble while driving downtown to yet another teacher/parent conference, he would also admit that being a fully engaged parent made him a richer human being. Dads need to share in both the glory and the tedium of parenting, or Mom would be designated the family's only homemaker. It doesn't always have to be 50/50, but if Dad were to disengage from active family participation, it would create a ripple effect, and the kids would then think it was okay to also duck out of the family circle.

Abigail knew that for her marriage to survive, it had to be a fair partnership. As it turned out, their partnership extended both ways. Although she was not a techie, Andrew's business needed Abby. Soon she was filling in at the office, and her counsel became essential, as it had been in her elite political job in DC. Just as Andrew worked to be active at home, Abby began actively working in his start-up tech business: their expanding corporation.

Soon Abigail's administrative and strategic skills began to fill in many of the blanks that the creative company sorely lacked. Their collective home/work paths has weathered a few bumps. It started small with Dad's waffles-and-eggs special and has grown into a dynamic, interconnected partnership where both spouses have found their valued calling and their best selves.

Reach-Out: STARS AND BUGS—AN INTERACTIVE ALLOWANCE SYSTEM.

Stars and Bugs is an allowance system my husband devised to get our children in the habit of tasks and rewards. Each child earns money in proportion to their level of contribution to the house and/or taking steps toward self-sufficiency. Stars and Bugs is a fun, pride-creating, and occasionally costly system, but it's worth it.

Stars are awarded for commissions completed and steps taken to work on challenges (in my youngest daughter's case, sleeping in her own bed). Bugs are a nicer way of saying "demerits."

Here's the chart I used when my daughter was 11 years old. It was personalized to her capabilities and quirks, but I made them—with mixed success—for all my children. This chart was hung on the refrigerator. My daughter was in charge of self-monitoring her Stars & Bugs. This system took some creative thought and time to set up and implement, but after that, it was up-and-running. It became a hit. Just know going in that this could cost 8–10 dollars a week but can save you half-an-hour a day of errands and work time. I call that a win/win.

Stars Vs. Bugs Billi's Allowance Sheet							Week of:_____ 4 ⁎ = $1		
STARS—Add $.25 each	Sunday	Monday	Tuesday	Wednesday	Thursday	Friday	Saturday	Total
• Make Bed • Teeth/Hair/Shower								
• Clothes in Hamper • Shoes & Clothes Away								
• Clean Bathroom • Empty Trash								
• Pick Up Toys & Books • Prepare Lunch								
• Make Breakfast • Help with Meals								
• Set the Table • Clear the Table								
• Clean Up After Meals • Load Dishwasher & Wash Dishes								
• Feed Dog • Walk Dog (2 Stars)								
• Prepare for Next Day Activities • Plan Own Play-dates								
• Sleep in Own Bed (4 Stars)								
BUGS—Subtract $.25 each	Sunday	Monday	Tuesday	Wednesday	Thursday	Friday	Saturday	Total
• Sleeping in Mom's Bed (2 Bugs) • Leaving Mess in Kitchen								
• Leaving Mess in Bedroom • Leaving Mess in Bathroom								
• Whining when Not Hurt • Meanness								

Total Stars: _____

Money Made: _____

*All *star* tasks will receive A single * unless otherwise noted.

Only parents can assign "bug" demerits . . . No sibling judges allowed.

Go to deborahjelinnewmyer.com to download and customize your own Stars Vs. Bugs charts for you own refrigerator!

Establishing an allowance system brings home to roost a smart work-for-money exchange system. Your kids can now experience the simple pleasure derived from being compensated with their own money, which might help them understand your desire to return to work and garner your own paycheck.

> ### Daily Do List
>
> ❑ Called a family meeting.
>
> ❑ Explained that everyone is getting a new job.
>
> ❑ Delegated age-appropriate tasks to kids and mate.
>
> ❑ Implemented a family allowance system.
>
> ❑ Kept up my to-do list and tidy-up minutes.

Hour Three
Calculate Your Finances

Ostriches Beware: Brace yourself for an eye-opening step. Knowing your budget is a must. This morning, double up on your caffeine dose, and let's estimate your **monthly nut.** You need to compute how much you are spending as a family. There are plenty of monthly budget guidelines you can download for free, but the simplest version I have come across is a model that just asks you to gather up your monthly bills to gauge your expenses. Without judgment, just total up the facts.

Reach-In Exercise: WHAT IS IN YOUR POCKETS?

Family Household Monthly Budget			
	Budget	Actual	Variance
Income			
Salary 1 (Take-Home Pay)			$ -
Salary 2 (Take-Home Pay)			-
Stocks/Bonds/Trusts			-
<Other Income>			-
Total Income			$ -
Expenses			
Fixed Costs			
Mortgage/Rent Expense			$ -
Car/Lease Payment(s)			-
Loan Payment(s)			-
Insurance - Health/Life			-
Insurance - Homeowner's/Car			-
Tuition/Summer Camp			-
Charitable Contributions			-
Childcare			-
Estimated Taxes			-
<Other Fixed Costs>			-
Total Fixed Costs			$ -

Semivariable Costs				
Water/Power/Gas			$	-
Telephone Expense				-
Cable/Satellite Television Expense				-
Internet Expense				-
Food (Dining Out & Groceries)				-
Gasoline				-
Pet Suppliers				-
Out of Network Heathcare				-
Personal Care				-
Final Tax Bill				-
<Other Semi Variable Costs>				
Total Semivariable Costs			$	-
Highly Variable Costs				
Entertainment			$	-
Gifts				-
Clothing				-
Miscellaneous				-
Travel and Vacations				-
<Other Highly Variable Costs>				-
Total Highly Variable Costs			$	-
Total Exepenses			$	-
Net Incomes			$	-

Maybe you have an accountant who helps you organize and pay some of these bills. No matter, take your head out of the financial sand. Know what you are spending. Be a grown-up and put that number firmly in your head. Having to live within a budget can be painful, but on the flip side, knowing how much you spend and how much you need to earn can also be liberating. It is only by knowing what you **spend** and what you **earn** that you can feel good about purchases. If you can remain in your budget, you will not have any guilt about indulgences every so often.

Do you know what your family income is now? Do you have solid financial literacy about the state of your bills, taxes, investments, retirement funds, health and life insurance costs, monthly cable subscription, all of those music apps your kids bought?

How Did SHE Do It?
She took control of her finance and became "wealthy enough."
Julie W., single mother of two teenage girls, freelance editor and writer.

Five years ago, Julie went through a mostly amicable divorce and was granted joint custody of her two daughters. When it was clear that her ex-husband was moving to another county—over an hour's drive away, it dawned on her that she was truly on her own. Her cushioning was gone, and she had to take control of her own finances. Before, when hers was a two-income family, dinners out or buying that new silk skirt was a nice treat. But now, she knows that if she wants to rent a paddleboard for an afternoon, she and the girls have to settle for leftovers for dinner. Everything became a budgeted trade-off. Her daughters could either travel with the club volleyball team for the summer or they could buy a ping-pong table for the backyard.

There are many financial tools at your disposal, but for Julie, she created a very basic route to financial control. She kept an old-school memo book in her wallet and wrote down everything she spent. Simple and definite. Julie's looks like this:

Date: _____   Item: _____   Amount _____

Monthly Tally _____

At the end of each month, Julie could transfer this information to a spreadsheet that told her exactly what she had spent—category by category. At first, this may have been arduous and painful, but now she knows her parameters, and becoming conscious of her spending gave her a new freedom. Not only was she less careless with her money, but, if a desired item was within her disposable cash budget, it became a guilt-free purchase. Also, Julie's financial clarity gave her confidence to advocate for her own salary worth. Once Julie took a close look at real costs in the real world, she became a more empowered negotiator for her own hourly rate.

Do you know what you want or need to earn at your new job in order for it to make financial sense for your family? I'm talking after benefits, net income. What's your number? Julie used a piece of paper in the side pocket of her purse. Many people swear by the helpful budgeting sites Mint.com or Smartbudget.com. Quicken also has a very user friendly version of budgeting (and paying bills). But as with any of these online expert advisors, you need to find the the one that works for you.

Financial clarity allows you to make smart decisions moving forward. It can sometimes dictate what type of job you look for, but it also gives infinite room to discover creative ways to earn an income that works for your family. Perhaps you would secure a more flexible part-time job to fill the monthly financial cup and still allow extra funds for indulgent self-care.

If you don't know what you have or need in the bank, you won't know what you need or want to earn. Start digging in. See what's there. If your spouse handles the finances, start to get into the fold and see what's incoming and outgoing. *If you know where you're short, you'll know what you need to earn.* Financial transparency and budgeting make everything easier.

How Did SHE Do It?
Against the statistical odds, she got stronger . . . and prevailed.
Elizabeth E., mother of two daughters, headmaster of an elite all-girls school

Today, Elizabeth is a respected icon in the girls' education movement and spends most of her day advocating young woman to "Play big and be fearless." But she was born without a silver spoon in sight, and her road to success demanded a lot of determined reinvention and buoyance.

Growing up in a large working-class family in New England, Elizabeth was the first to graduate from college, which might have been enough. Then, she channeled her love for literature into teaching and spent many happy years as a talented high school English teacher . . . and that might have been enough. However, once she dug into her own maturing ambition and mixed in her desire to push others beyond their standings, she knew she wanted more. Elizabeth went back to school and got an Educational Masters in Leadership from Harvard and applied for several Headmaster positions up and down the East Coast. Sadly, and yet another crummy statistic, even though less than 25 percent of the people who work in schools are men, 75 percent of the Principals/Headmasters are men.

Elizabeth butted up against this statistic for many years, and even though she was frustrated by the traditional biases—especially when less qualified men got the job—she never became resentful. She just kept advocating for herself and specifically for girls' education. She kept aiming high. She kept playing big. She became proud when she was labeled an "elegant feminist" and wore her "bad-ass" badge as a triumph. And now, after years in the trenches, she is Head of School for a prestigious girls' school in California. She is passionate and devoted to girls fulfilling their potential, and she often writes and speaks out about education, parenting, and issues facing modern girls today.

For Elizabeth, one hidden pitfall to girls' empowerment is their own "financial illiteracy." Too often, girls are not taught about money. Or worse, they are told it is gauche to speak about money. Financial ignorance stifles women's power, both in business and at home. And yet, practical finance is too often overlooked in even the best academic schools. Elizabeth is a big proponent of financial fearlessness and has struggled to integrate financial literary classes in her school's curriculum.

As many women have discovered too often when asked about finances, they sheepishly default to an "I don't know" stance or feel it is somehow impolite to talk about money. Let's de-stigmatize discussions about money and make sure our next generation goes out into the world having learned the basics of personal business.

Daily Do List

☐ Calculated my finances.

☐ Petitioned my child/children's school(s) for a financial literacy elective.

Hour Four
Update Your Social Media
(No Freaking Out Allowed)

Are the above icons hieroglyphics or a new fun fashion?

Do these symbols induce a panic attack or colorful joy?

Face it, social media has become part of daily life, but many in the mom generation still may avoid these doodads, while some are on the cutting edge of the digital globe. Plenty of my friends brag that they do not have a Facebook or Instagram account.

I find the web world stimulating and entertaining, but still I am often stumped by the "new math" of the Internet's portals and functions. There are options at my fingertips that reach beyond where I ever wanted to go.

Yet, like it or not, if you want to get a job in today's market, you have to embrace the digital jungle. Nowadays, so much information is dispatched . . . So many connections are made exclusively online. So if you don't have profiles on Facebook and LinkedIn, it's time to get crackin'! Those two are your biggest allies in your job searches and networking. Also, if you really want to keep up and let potential employers get to know you, an Instagram and Twitter profile would also be helpful. If you already have profiles, it's time to upgrade them to professional status.

Reach-Out: YOUR PROFESSIONAL PROFILE.

It's now universal that employers look at potential employees' social media profiles. Why wouldn't they? It's an easy look into you and your life, right there in front of them! Even as you warn your children about the dangers of social media, you also need to remind yourself that anything that goes on the Internet is *forever* on the Internet. So from now

Continued . . .

---

on, if you aren't already, be discretionary about the content you allow on your profiles. So you got a little tipsier than you meant to at last year's college reunion? Who cares—I'm not judging (I probably would have been right there clinking glasses and pushing shots), but those rosy cheeks and the squinty smile don't give the impression of you as a together, with-it, responsible employee. That photo goes!

Perhaps your guilty pleasure is unwinding with a marathon of The Real Housewives. Again, no judgment! But perhaps listing it as your favorite show is a little TMI for the picture you're trying to paint of yourself. When in doubt, take it down. Still, stay you! Don't make your profile boring and without personality—you still want it to accurately represent you in all your unique glory. Just think: *friendly, active, appropriate.*

LinkedIn is a little easier than other sites because it's specifically geared toward the working professional. Make sure to use a photo that's current, professional, and where you're *smiling.* Then, upload your work experience and look for all possible connections. You want to grow your online network; start now with user-kind LinkedIn. Check which working Facebook friends are on LinkedIn, and connect with them. Look for all the friends on that list you made in Step 2, and find the people who own businesses you like and respect around town.

This is also a great way to begin a connection with someone who intimidates you a little (or a lot). It's way less scary to click a button than it is to pick up the phone (at first; phone calls will follow, just FYI)! And this way, when you inevitably dare yourself to pick up the phone (you daredevil), you will have already planted the seed.

Reach-In Exercise: SCHEDULE A SOCIAL MEDIA UPDATE DATE.

Spend ten minutes every day tending to the business of your social media accounts. Schedule this as a cyber maintenance habit . . . ten minutes only. Do not just wander online whenever and take a quick Buzzfeed quiz or check out your daughter's Pinterest wedding board. Discipline yourself with this valuable digital tool. Every day check in with your accounts. Make sure your profiles are clean and updated. Scan the "People you Know" vertical, and request three or four names you may have forgotten into your Career Contact Web.

Reach-Out: CREATE A SKYPE ACCOUNT.

This is the last bit of technology I'm going to ask you to interact with today. Many interviews are now conducted via Skype (or the less official iPhone Facetime or Facebook's Video Chat). It's more efficient for employers and, frankly, more efficient for you since you don't have to drive anywhere. There is absolutely something to be said for being in the same room and shaking someone's hand, but this seems to be the interview method of the world now. Some interviews will still be in person, but enough are over Skype that you need to familiarize yourself with the program now so you don't flounder trying to figure it out the morning of your first interview!

Go to Skype.com and create an account. Use the same photo that you used on Facebook and/or LinkedIn, and find a friend or text your brother to schedule a practice call with them so you can learn the bells and whistles (there really aren't many, but you don't want to get tripped up in an interview). Helpful tip: decide ahead of time who is calling whom, and from what time zone. I've had numerous botched experiences where I've scheduled a call with someone for 4 p.m. EST. That time rolls around and nothing happens because we're both sitting at our computers thinking the other hasn't called because she isn't ready. So make sure you double-check the time zone of the person you're calling, and make sure you're both clear on who's doing the actual calling.

Skype and FaceTime are so important. Make sure you're being consistent in your organizational and interpersonal habits.

Daily Do List

❏ Created or updated my social media profile; . . . at very least reviewed Facebook and LinkedIn.

❏ Created and tested my Skype account.

❏ Reminded myself that I don't have to do everything.

❏ Kept delegating tasks to fellow housemates.

❏ Searched professional websites for new contacts, ten minutes per day.

Hour Five
Artfully Begin "The Ask"

There is one in every family . . . that adorable kid who seems to always get everything she wants. The mythology in most large families is that the older siblings and cousins pave the way, and the parents get progressively looser and more generous as the younger ones grow up.

One particular cousin, Willa, seemed to have been born into the family's sweet spot and somehow, after years of wanting a family dog . . . when Willa asked, Nellie-the-dog was brought home. Somehow, Willa was always the one to use the family's phone upgrade. Somehow, while still in high school, Willa convinced her mom to go on a mother-daughter safari trip to Africa. Willa got all the perks. The running cousins' joke was, "How did Willa get those new elite Soccer Cleats?" The truest answer was always "She asked."

Of course, everyone's expectation was that Willa would be ruined by her mom's indulgences, and she would never be able to fend for herself. In fact, she grew into an intensely driven and independent adult who, at a very early age, studied her older siblings' attempts and developed an expert ability *to ask*.

Turns out she wasn't just being bratty. Instead, Willa figured out how to be assertively charming and confident. She always managed to back up her "ask" with a convincing rationale that didn't mean she was "special"; rather, she felt she was worthy of the ask. She always made the favor you would be doing her seem it was a win for you, too. Who wouldn't take pleasure in a bonus trip with your gracious and appreciative offspring? With tremendous savvy, Willa could pinpoint and articulate her ask with such an easy charm that made the giver want to give. For years, she pitched her "asks" to her parents, but soon Willa learned how to ask teachers, ask bosses, and ask friends. Good for Willa.

How Did SHE Do It?
She asked. Period.

Dr. Monica S., mother of two boys and full-time concierge doctor, Burbank, CA

Monica was a respected internist with a prestigious Los Angeles medical group, and her husband, Bryan, worked in finance. She loved being a doctor, and she was good at it. She never wanted anybody else raising her kids, so she and her husband planned ahead. With some trepidation, she approached her medical group to change her hours when she returned from maternity leave. Monica would leave her home before 6:00 a.m., completing her rounds at the hospital before seeing her first patient at at 7:00 a.m. in the office. Then she would work through lunch and leave at 2:00 p.m. to ALWAYS pick her boys up from school. She would leave the house ALWAYS while everyone was still sleeping, and her husband was ALWAYS in charge of readying the boys and getting them to school by 8:45 a.m., nearly three hours into Monica's workday. At first, the management group was skeptical of Monica's plan but gave her a six-month trial for this newly invented early shift. As it turned out, plenty of patients clamored to schedule appointments early. They, too, wanted this pre-9 a.m. option, and the demand for this seemingly radical idea grew. Since then, other doctors followed and have also shifted their hours earlier. This turned out to be a win-win, but if Monica had not spoken up with a coparenting plan, she may have eventually opted-out of her medical career in favor of her kids' well-being.

It surprised Monica that the medical industry was able to be flexible. However, they could never had said yes if she hadn't asked. Still, there are challenges with the reality of this early morning schedule. There are whole segments of her kids' childhood that Monica is missing. But, something had to be sacrificed to manage a full life and a full career. And by most accounts, Monica can claim a solid victory for herself and for others' juggling. The moral of the story is: always, always *ask*.

"Asking" is a muscle. Let's begin stretching and pumping that muscle. You have spent the last few weeks becoming a capable job candidate; now let's make the final push and psych yourself to ASK. If twenty-year-old Willa can figure out how to ask, what are you waiting for? Go out there and get that puppy, that iPhone upgrade, and that new ideal job.

Asking is not easy, and, statistically, you are not alone. In Hewitt's study mentioned earlier, "54% of off-ramped woman left their job without even discussing flex options with their supervisors."

Perhaps I had spent too many hours listening to the soundtrack of Oliver, or I was too afraid of of rejection, but for much of my career I dreaded reaching out to my bosses and asking, "Please sir, can I have some more." I thought my hard work would magically be appreciated and rewarded. Dream on.

Likewise, I would often duck away from fundraising committees; I'd sooner write a personal check than ask someone else to write one for my cause. "Asking" never came naturally; in fact, I would have listed asking one of my fears. I always presumed I would get a no, so I avoided any chance of rejection. Then I realized a no wasn't going to really hurt me. And if I could frame the ask properly, I might even get a yes. As my career and life shifted, I had to force myself to become a *better asker*. And as my confidence grew, so, too, did my sense of worthy entitlement. I became a better salesperson and more proficient at advocating for myself.

HOW TO ASK: Cheat Sheet:

Be Brave Enough to ASK.

I honestly believe that human beings want to help other human beings. Being generous feels good. Doing favors for others feeds the karma jar and your soul, and often makes one feel lucky that they are able to help out. Not everyone has the time or the power or the bandwidth to truly help, but I am satisfied with a 3:1 ask:receive ratio. And keep a log of to whom you reached out and when. Refer to the "Contacts & Connections" tracker on page 61. Use it, then follow up. Don't think too long and hard about the ask; that's just fear. Tell your fear, "thank-you-very-much, but I'm asking anyway." Remember, you can be brave and afraid at the same time.

It's possibly also true that asking a friend is harder for you than cold-asking a stranger. That's okay, too. Either way, bolster yourself and commit to making three outgoing efforts a day: a phone call, email, or text to someone in your desired industry.

- Ask with specific clarity. Don't say I am looking for "a change" and expect the other person to figure out your ask.
- Ask with a doable request that the helper is able to accomplish.
- Make sure the request is an easy, one step ask: If you want a letter forwarded, make sure it is already attached to your original note.

The Determined Ask: Tenacity Matters

Eighty-five percent of all incoming calls are unsolicited cold calls. Often it is for something I have no interest in: carpet cleaning deals, switching to a new cellphone carrier, a solar panel estimate. But even for causes that I care about—Police Benevolence Society, Planned Parenthood, an upcoming election—I personally hate the interruption that phone calls make in my home. Even though I have tried to block these unwanted calls, still, the phone keeps ringing. Often, as soon as I hear that unsolicited call pause, and before they mispronounce my last name, I quietly hang up. Sometimes I hang on long enough to beg the caller to "Please, please take me off your list." Still, the phone keeps on ringing.

However annoying they may be, the cold call industry must be working; so many companies rely on these centers. And you have to marvel at their cold-calling persistence. Hang up after hang up, they continue to make "The Ask."

Reach-Out Exercise: JUMP OUT OF YOUR COMFORT ZONE.

Although it might seem like a nightmare, it might be helpful to join a phone bank for one day. Push yourself into the cold-call world. Witness how others ask—even if it is a scripted ask. Train yourself to overcome phone insecurity and master tenacity. Today, let's promise yourself to do something that makes you uncomfortable, such as:

- Say "Yes" to an invite that may be awkward.
- Invite someone else to go to an event.
- Volunteer to fundraise for your school.
- Join a phone bank for a political committee—they always need help, and they are always hung up on.

"Discomfort creates resilience."
—Jocelyn Solomon, popular yoga sage

Reframe The Ask Into a Fun Challenge.

A few years ago, I was fortunate enough to meet with the president of my kid's university. I asked him how he managed to not completely dread the constant task of fundraising. At every stop on a college president's schedule, his job is to ask for money. Surprisingly, this president admitted he liked "the ask." This was a revelation.

"Yes, my mission is always somewhat mercenary: to get the person sitting across from me to write a check to the college. But for me, the challenge is to find the nugget of reward I can offer in return. I never want them to feel like it's a one-way street. Thus, I describe how their check will accomplish something specific and worthy. As often as possible, I avoid using 'guilt' or 'obligation' as part of my ask."

Mr. College President understood that if he could propose a cause/effect reward to their gift, they would actually enjoy giving.

He reframed his task of fundraising into the creative tournament of turning *his ask* into a *welcomed opportunity for the giver*. At the time, it seemed like a career rationale and a neat party trick . . . but at the core of that advice is the key to *The Ask: If you know the right way to ask, people want to give*. Likewise, if you've taken the steps to become a good job candidate, a boss will want to hire you.

Asking takes bravery and confidence. And sadly, especially when you are out on a limb looking for work, both bravery and confidence are in short supply—sometimes, you have to fake it.

No one likes difficult homework; it is always easier to distract yourself with a YouTube video or tackle Sunday's *New York Times* crossword, but don't let yourself be distracted by the fear of asking. Grab your to-do list. Reopen your Connections and Contacts Tracker from page 61 and get brave.

For me, my biggest insecurity wells up with the second ask. Maybe I floated an initial request, then . . . crickets. Asking again might seem like nagging, but still, the only way you are going to find rewarding work is to:

- Write another cover letter (switch it up a little).
- Make another phone call.
- Follow up on an alternate lead.
- Get yourself invited to another informational interview.

The Ask Recap: First, Find *THE RIGHT ASK* for *THE RIGHT PERSON*.
Most people are willing to do "a solid" if it is easy and the request is clear.

- Make three new outgoing reaches a day, online or via the phone.
- Write a follow-up to two previous "asks"—"The Double Ask."

- Place at least one "ask" phone call.
- Log it all down in your Contacts and Connections List.
- DO make it feel like flattery to the person you are asking.
- DON'T overask or expect them to figure out what you want to do. Know before you go. Keep the ask specific. Keep it simple and one step.
- If you admire someone's job and they have a career you envy, ask for an informational meeting at their office. DON'T ask her to find you a position at her company. And always end the meeting with a suggestion of another informational meeting with somebody else. And DON'T forget a gracious "thank you," of course.
- If you are interested in a career in yoga, DO ask your favorite teacher how she became a teacher. DON'T ask anyone to get you a job; instead, ask them to tell you about their path to job happiness. Listen and get inspired.
- And then if you hear about a legit job opening, be direct. DO ASK for that specific job. Throw your hat in the ring with confidence, charm, and entitlement. Even if the experience requirements don't exactly match your "transferable skills," apply anyway.
- And then snoop around and ASK anyone who knows anything about that specific job opening to put in a good word for you.

There are all sorts of "asks":

- The Cover Letter Ask: Charming and distinctive. But make it crystal clear what you want.
- The Phone Call Follow-up Ask: First try to make sure they got your cover letter. Then, phone call to set a face to face.
- The Clever Ask: Befriend the assistant (they have more power than you think).
- The Direct-without-stalking Ask: Be charming. Self-effacing. But determined.

"Don't look down, look ahead."
—Nancy Driver, college counselor

The Pre-ask Exercise: Begin Naming Names

Next week, you will begin applying for real, specific jobs. Reach for the stars, but give those stars a name. You might wish for a job in several different categories, but be specific about your target. It could be working at Trader Joe's or UCLA Admissions, or for Jeff Bezos. However impossible the reach, just spew out your fantasy, but give each ideal a legit name.

For example, if I want to work as a consultant in the health industry, what are the five places that service hospitals, doctors, clinics?

Five fantastic companies . . . give them a name:

1. _____

2. _____

3. _____

4. _____

5. _____

Five dream bosses I would love to work for:

1. _____

2. _____

3. _____

4. _____

5. _____

Five people who have the job I want:

1. _____

2. _____

3. _____

4. _____

5. _____

PART II
YOU ARE READY: NOW GO OUT AND WIN THAT JOB.

Step Five
BE THE IDEAL CANDIDATE

You're done looking back. You've marginalized your regrets. You've shaken off your out-of-work cobwebs and are ready to be an attractive hire. This is the week you will brand yourself as a fabulous candidate, while you build an eye-catching résumé and cover letter. You will scout helpful tidbits about the specific job you covet.

This week, we will add to that a list of the companies, stores, or people you want to be in business with. Take that list and research each source. Then, unleash your lioness within and practice your elevator pitch, portal out your résumé, cover letter, optimistic energy, and charm. Sounds good . . . Let's go.

Hour Goals

Hour One:	Create your résumé & update your digital footprint.
Hour Two:	List your top Fave Five jobs and best contacts.
Hour Three:	Practice and preach your elevator pitch.
Hour Four:	Write a spirited cover letter template.
Hour Five:	Apply! Apply! Apply!

Hour One
Get Crackin' on Your Résumé

Link Yourself to LinkedIn.

Honestly, it is not easy (or usually fun) to write your résumé. Too bad. It requires introspection and articulation, and sometimes dredges up feelings of regret and inadequacy. I feel your pain and understand why it's easy to avoid writing one at all, but the only way to get your résumé written is to sit down and write it. Excuses and distractions are like weeds: turn off all your cyber contacts and set your web blockers for the following hour. Focus, girlfriend.

I thought it was only fair that I, too, sit down to grind out my own résumé. Like many of you, I hadn't worked in a résumé-driven world, so for years I could get by with a bio or a list of my most recent credits. Then, when I wanted to join LinkedIn, I needed to create a more traditional document. We all need to get on LinkedIn. Their steps for starting your career are extremely user-friendly, and their outreach is spectacular.

It can be difficult to find enough "brag-able" loglines about yourself but there are countless services, sites, and samples online to help you build your new résumé. I have found they were all pretty similar and offered fill-in-the-blanks templates that can help you get started.

Even if none of these online sites take you all the way home, they will lift you over a few speed bumps and launch you into your résumé writing. My trick was to pretend I was taking a fun BuzzFeed quiz or filling out a Bumble questionnaire, and with those breezier end games in mind, creating my résumé took on a livelier tone. And my résumé turned out to be unique and spirited.

Résumé Cheat Sheet

If the LinkedIn plug-in résumé doesn't work for you, my two favorite sites for building a résumé with style and support are:

LIVE CAREER | http://www.livecareer.com/resume-builder

RESUME GENIUS | https://resumegenius.com/

Sit down at your now-tidy desk, check out these sites, and spend an hour creating a formal résumé. You probably won't get it all done today, but with focus, you can get plenty completed. Starting is the key. Résumés are always evolving, but give yourself a deadline, say, the end of the week, to have something submittable.

In my experience as an employer and looking at hundreds of résumés that have crossed my desk, I have plenty of opinions as to what makes a fantastic résumé. You can scan the web for other helpful hints, but as a potential employer, when I pick up a résumé, I like to see the following:

- Graphically easy-to-read with bolded highlights and categories.
- Only list your most impressive experiences. Skip your duds.
- No lies. Ever. And yet, it's definitely okay to enhance your experiences. If you were a part-time ski instructor that winter, your first love broke your heart, and were too depressed to do anything but ski, wear it proudly. Just don't call yourself "ski bum."
- At least one nonprofessional brag. Provide a passionate conversation starter. As an interviewer, I was always happy to talk about your pilot's license or your ivy-league degree in mixology.
- One page is all you need. Always try to fit everything onto a single sheet. Sometimes that means having a different résumé for different job prospects and positions.
- Always keep a ream of nice paper around to print out your résumé and cover letter. Even though many résumés are formulated online as a PDF, always have a printed copy on hand. Linen is good. Don't scrimp.

Fill 'Er Up

As an off-ramped mom, you may have spent many work-hours or many work-years out of the traditional workforce. But however scenic your route may appear, you have not been idle. Your challenge will be to find résumé filler that attractively describes your time-out. There are several schools of thought on how to describe your years off the work highway: 1) Do not try to hide your time away; 2) Do not try to convince an employer that being on the PTA Board is the same as sitting at the weekly executive staff meetings; 3) Cop to the fact that your off-ramp/job switch may have taken you down a notch—in advancement and salary—but you still and again have plenty to offer; 4) You know you will have to prove yourself. . . . You are expecting that your commitment and your talent will be on trial.

Résumé No-Nos

- Telling Your Life Story. Avoid padding the résumé by listing too many hobbies, religious affiliations, and family status. Some random employer might very well care about your rescued parakeet from South America, but not as much as you do. Dial it down.
- A novel . . . or even a novella. Always keep your résumé to one page. More than one page shows a lack of professionalism and, more important, someone who may not have a solid grasp of the social boundaries appropriate to the work environment. That job you had at an ice cream stand on the boardwalk in seventh grade was a great start to a flourishing career, but now that you're forty plus, you can safely leave it behind.
- Revolving doors. Unless it was set up as a freelance project accomplishment, don't even bother to list a corporate job that lasted less than six months.

Adjectives Abound; Action Verbs Sell

Be generous with synonyms, descriptive words, and active verbs. Even if you "handled" a million things and "compiled" a lot of stuff, use other words to describe the same task, or it gets to sound ridiculous. Here's a helpful list of words that are just like other words, but . . . different. Variety helps keep your résumé alive.

Résumé Writing Action Verb List

Always use action verbs, not "duties include" or "responsible for." Additionally, represent your duties as professionally and accurately as possible. Do not misrepresent them.

COMMUNICATIONS

acted as liaison	consulted	informed	moderated	referred
advised	corresponded	instructed	negotiated	sold
advocated	counseled	interfaced	notified	synergized
arbitrated	curated	interpreted	presented	trained
authored	demonstrated	interviewed	promoted	translated
connected	displayed	lectured	publicized	wrote
convened	edited	marketed	published	
commented	guided	mediated	recommended	

ADMINISTRATION

administered	determined	initiated	organized	represented
appointed	directed	instituted	overhauled	revamped
arranged	dispensed	issued	oversaw	reviewed
completed	distributed	launched	prescribed	routed
conducted	diversified	managed	presided	selected
consolidated	executed	motivated	provided	supervised
contracted	founded	obtained	recruited	supplied
controlled	governed	offered	rectified	terminated
coordinated	headed	opened	referred	trained
delegated	implemented	ordered	regulated	

PLANNING AND DEVELOPMENT

broadened	devised	improved	planned
created	discovered	initiated	prepared
designed	drafted	invented	produced
developed	estimated	modified	proposed

ANALYSIS

amplified	computed	examined	investigated	studied
analyzed	detected	forecasted	programmed	systemized
calculated	diagnosed	formulated	researched	tested
compiled	evaluated	identified (needs)	solved	

FINANCIAL/RECORDS MANAGEMENT

audited	collected	invested	minimized	reconciled
allocated	condensed	inventoried	monitored	recorded
balanced	documented	listed	processed	scheduled
catalogued	expedited	logged	procured	traced
charted	guaranteed	maximized	purchased	updated

MANUAL

assembled	delivered	maintained	repaired	rewired
built	designed	navigated	replaced	tested
constructed	installed	operated	restored	trimmed

Hiring a Résumé Helper.

If you're stumped and cannot find the discipline to pump yourself up and fill in your best blank spots, there are plenty of good, private résumé pros who could coach you through this step. Usually they cost between $300–500, and, nowadays, they will also help you with an elegant cover letter and snappy LinkedIn page.

Anybody you hire to build your résumé needs to be your front-line salesperson, so vet their work. Make sure they have great samples that appeal to you, and check off the following important qualities:

1. They get to know you and have a real sense of what you have to offer.
2. Understand the industry to which you're applying.
3. Can emphasize your achievements in a modern context.

Keep Updating Your Social Media Accounts.

Your résumé and cover letter are just the beginning of your to-do list. You also need to maintain your digital profiles, but do NOT make updating and snooping a full-time hobby.

Double-clean your Facebook account. It is the first thing HR departments or potential employers look at. Get rid of those pictures of you eating double chocolate cake and twerk dancing at the bowling alley. Avoid political, crazy-person rants. Beware of the inappropriate comments about people, places, and things. If you think a particular post is a marginal call, toss it out.

Once you have a résumé, your LinkedIn profile is simply a cut and paste job. This mini-version of your résumé puts you out into the marketplace. It's a most valuable trolling tool for you and for various employers. It's the Facebook of the work world, a career and networking hub for you to jumpstart your next chapter. It could possibly land you a job. Don't take it lightly.

If you have a special talent that makes you proud, you might consider posting your video résumé on YouTube. Again, though, like your Facebook profile and pictures, make sure you do not have anything off-color or incriminating on public display.

Keep scanning your social media for job-intel and to discover new potential contacts:

- Facebook Profile
- LinkedIn Profile
- Instagram and Twitter
- Pinterest and Tumblr

Daily Do List

❑ Started my résumé (did-it-myself OR hired an expert).

❑ Sent three emails today. Started my habit of asking my Contacts & Connections.

❑ Updated my social media profiles.

❑ Double-checked my various Post-it notes and To-dos. Tossed out what I've completed.

Hour Two
Naming Your Best-Case Scenarios

Our mission by the end of this step is to apply to *at least* five jobs. To accomplish this goal, you first need to pinpoint your personal Fave Five occupations, companies, etc., where you would love to work—pick a latitude and longitude and start digging. Giving a name to your wish list is always the best first step to define your prospects.

> " *You've got to be very careful if you don't know where you're going, because you might not get there.* "
> —Yogi Berra

Reach-In Exercise: DECLARE YOUR FAVORITE FAVE FIVE.

The very best way to score a dream job is to name it. Be specific. What would be your *Most Wanted* landing spot? Oddly, this critical exercise is often tougher than it seems. Today you need to actualize your ideal job by admitting its name, its address, and a point person. Aim high. Be specific.

My Fave Five Occupations and Why
I would succeed the best in this specific field:

1. _____

2. _____

3. _____

4. _____

5. _____

Continued . . .

My Fave Five Companies

I want to get a job at this specific type of company (retail, corporate, mom & pop, etc.):

1. _____

2. _____

3. _____

4. _____

5. _____

Now You Need To:

- Explore their website. And see what they are listing as job opportunities.
- Figure out exact emails and mailing addresses for the boss you want.
- Track down their Human Resources (HR) manager or company recruiter (or the temp company that services them).
- Refer back to your FaceBook and LinkedIn Contacts and Connections and see if anybody knows anybody who works there. Or has any intel on your ideal company.
- Investigate deeper and become an expert in the company's history, work policies, and future strategies.
- Ask all your friends if they know anybody working at your ideal job sites. Get your foot in the door.
- Even if there is not an available job opening, make sure the Recruiter or HR person likes you. Make new friends everywhere you can.

After you have named your preferred companies, now check their websites. Many companies post jobs directly on their sites. Go to the vertical pull-down markers and look for "job opportunities," "careers," etc. In many cases (even if they want to hire internally), HR is required to list open positions. Sometimes that exact job no longer exists, but still, your foothold is getting somewhere.

Perhaps one of those Fave Fives might have future openings that are not yet listed, and you will have made a mark into their system. Perhaps someone brought their best friend, who used to work for eBay, to a barbeque. You are a frequenter of eBay and heard about an opening there. Say something! This is the time to yank out your moxie.

By the end of the week, you'll have pushed your name and résumé out into these specific places.

If you're looking for something not so corporate, be innovative about how to land your less conventional dream job:

- If you want to write short stories, what are the *Fave Five* publications and addresses for your most favorite, fabulous places where you'd want to see your writing featured?
- If you want to become a therapist, what are the five most fabulous grad schools in your area, or top-ranked online options?
- If you want to become a florist, what are your *Fave Five* floral boutiques?
- If you want to become a professional photographer, what are your Fave Five art galleries, local photographers, framing stores, and restaurants that showcase and sell art?

Even though these smaller companies may not have a recruiting department, get as much contact information from them as possible. And even if they do not have a job opening, send them an inquiry. Drop off a résumé. Put yourself out for the specific place you want to inhabit. Do everything you can to get an inside look at your Fave Five opportunities. Even if you never make it past the receptionist or the HR interview, the more you see about the brick-and-mortar space you want to inhabit, the better. An inside-the-door peek can tell you what you want and don't want moving forward.

Fave Five Inspirational Leaders
These men and women inspire me and I would love to be mentored by them:

1. _____

2. _____

3. _____

4. _____

5. _____

Name a particular employer whom you'd want to hire you. This could be a maverick businessman, bar owner, musician, environmental trailblazer, etc. Find and figure out their email. Write them directly, or scout your contacts for a referral. If they work at a larger company, also pursue them via their recruiting or HR department.

Fave Five Offices, Stores, or Boutiques

1. _____

2. _____

3. _____

4. _____

5. _____

The more specific you can be, the easier it is to get it done. Chances are you won't land a VP of Marketing spot at a top entertainment firm right away (unless that's always been in your career bag and you've worked up to it), but once you name your ideal job, very often a facsimile of that job is within your reach. You might need to restart your career in an entry-level situation, for less money or reduced benefits; or you might need to work for another company that is on an emerging tier to your dream company. Don't be discouraged by the gate or the gatekeeper; get excited! This is an exercise in getting laser-focused about what you are willing to work for.

Food for Thought:

Fran Helm, a technology, media, and telecommunications recruiter for the Spencer Stuart executive search firm, said, "Seventy percent of jobs never get listed. Most jobs come from internal promotions, personal or professional rolodexes, and who you know or who your friends know matters."

Reach-In Exercise: YOUR PICTURE FRAME.

Here's a fun suggestion I heard about a female business leader that is worth sharing. Nancy is now a happily retired grandparent, but not too long ago she led several global corporations and two television networks. Still, her most valued divining rod for her own business future was a simple and small empty picture frame. She would carry that frame with her and always ponder what image would best fill her empty frame: celebrity handshake photos; her backyard rose garden; her honorary awards; her nine grandchildren; a paycheck stub; an offer from another struggling corporation she might fix; her fiftieth wedding anniversary.

What do you want in your empty picture frame? Try it. Close your eyes and imagine a photograph that shows you in your most ideal light. What would tomorrow's perfect picture be for you?

- Giving a TED Talk with your family sitting in the front row?
- Mid-flight in your business-class seat, heading to Bali to scout locations for a new hotel chain ?
- At home in your comfy clogs, coaching a client via Skype, with your baby napping in the next room?
- In your backyard studio designing next year's line of eco-friendly jewelry?
- Relishing the nice tan from the vacation you just took with your family?

For me, it was easy to find today's *picture frame*: It was always my family holiday card.

My future picture frame was a little harder to fill, as it was often a dream-in-motion. Perhaps it is the final, approved cover for this book, or me around a teak table strategizing careers with friends, or producing another movie project, or four ticket stubs to *Hamilton*. I keep my frame with a rotating picture. Nowadays, people can rotate their computer desktop photo, or change their Facebook profile picture regularly. If you are comfortable with the public reveals that can add an element of social networking, then use your Facebook or Instagram as your ideal picture frame to strut your status.

For my old-school self, the empty picture frame sitting on my neat desk is an exceedingly great tool. If you don't dream in photographic images, you could write out your parameters for a future perfect job. Sometimes I write out my wannabe job quest and put them in a picture frame where I can gaze at it everyday.

IDEAL JOB :

- **A lively work atmosphere.**
- **An office where I'm not going to be the one in charge, but an appreciated cog in the grander agenda.**
- **A boss** who is a **buyer** with some weight/money/power and needs a **classy content/scout developer.**
- **A boss/leader** who respects:
    My confident intelligence
    My grit and strategic mind/play
    My connections, experience, and reputation
    (. . . and someone who gets my jokes)

So what is in your picture frame? What's the image you are most happy to brag about? Go through your selfies, your Facebook images, your vision map, or Pinterest. Fill this frame and keep it in your line of sight as you proceed through the next weeks of your *Mom for Hire* climb.

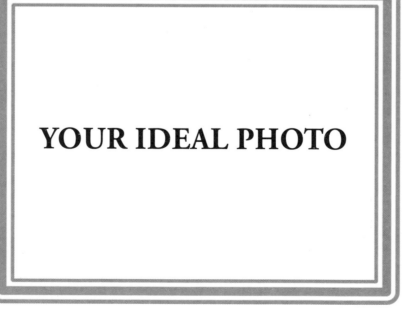

> *"I am so bad-ass!"*
> —Melissa McCarthy in *Spy*

. . . as she is jumping over a team of construction workers on an exhilarating car chase through Rome and she lands her Vespa in a puddle of hardening cement.

There is no exact science to finding the right match for your next chapter. Many, many paths can lead to satisfying work, and there are plenty of variables along the way. Never giving up—stick-to-itiveness—is key. Luck is also a factor. Right place, right time is nice but cannot be counted on. My grandfather, who emigrated penniless from the Ukraine to Hoboken, NJ, at age six, and died a very wealthy man, loved telling his rags-to-riches story to anyone who would listen. As a kid he would pick up coal that fell off a train speeding by his house. One day while hustling a coal sale, he overheard about a neighborhood house being for sale. The lightbulb went off: "Selling is Selling" . . . It was 1906, and he convinced his sister to loan him $6, he bought a desk, and he became the youngest realtor in Hudson County. Even when I was a little girl, his mantra that most stuck with me was "The harder I work, the luckier I get."

Giving up is not an option. This job hunt might easily take longer than you would like and will likely be tainted by rejection. But keep on looking for your professional match.

Daily Do List

❑ Listed my Fave Five.

❑ Gathered their specific contact information.

❑ Researched their gatekeeping filters to make contact.

❑ Strategized with Core Four (and beyond) and any helpful contacts.

❑ Repolished my résumé

How Did SHE Do It?
First she followed tradition, then she followed her dream.

*Jamie C., mother of two, advertising executive, summer
camp co-owner, and marketing executive*

Before spinning became a national sport, Jamie moonlighted as the most kick-ass spinning sergeant at the sportiest gym in Cleveland, Ohio. Throughout her twenties, she impressed her colleague at a sports & branding agency headquartered in Cleveland with her strategic spark, her candor, and awesome abs. Jamie worked full-time plus in marketing media for the motor sports division, and because of her clear, sometimes biting judgments, she was the darling of all the Grand Prix racers. A pretty dazzling early career.

Jamie's more traditional mother, however, did not raise her to be a "careerist." Mom was emphatic that if Jamie wanted to have kids, her working pace would have to slow down and she had to shift her focus to the home. Jamie followed her mom's advice without resentment and downsized her ambition and her workweek. Jamie found a way to keep her "foot in the door" by working at a local advertising agency, fewer hours and without travel, but it was not ideal. Oh well, her daughters were delightful, and she could always spin.

When her husband became co-owner of a New England summer camp, Jamie became the mistress of "camp." She overhauled the camp kitchen to be both delicious and healthy, she put the girl power back in the girls' camp, and added a theater barn for expanded arts programming to benefit both boys and girls. And—of course—she bought 10 spinning bicycles. Jamie was still Jamie. And always found ways to be a proactive impact player. She found a way to put the dormant camp to great use for a week in September by producing an empowering women's retreat. It was during this retreat that Jamie realized that her work at camp had become a stadium-sized version of running their home back in Cleveland.

Instead of two kids and a husband to manage, she now had 450 kids and 180 acres in the White Mountains of New Hampshire. And yet, after a decade making the best of corunning a camp, she felt she was pushing her husband's rocks up the hill.

So she went home to Ohio to find a full-time job she could call her own. A job that would compensate her with her own paycheck. Headhunters were very

Continued . . .

discouraging, and although she looked youthful and was still great in a room, she was warned that she had leaned out for too long to ever be considered. Still, she kept networking. It was hard to convince men that she really wanted to go back to work. Also, Cleveland was not a huge city, and her options were not infinite, but she had a dream picture of her future self, "Jamie: the independent business woman." Juggling calls with clients, creating pitches, and strategizing in staff meetings. Finally, she envisioned herself coming home after dark, to a meal lovingly cooked by her capable husband and teenage girls.

Jamie held onto this ideal image to fuel her year-long job hunt, and she weathered the rejections. Instead of giving up, she double-focused her efforts and kept boldly "branding" herself with assertive and pithy charm. Dejected, but undeterred, she reached out to over thirty potential resources. Finally, she had lunch with an acquaintance she had volunteered with twenty years prior, who now ran a local, respected advertising firm. After jumping through a few hoops, he offered her a chance. She took a pay cut and buckled down for a trial period in which she was going to have to earn credibility. Her kids missed her easy availability and were not always supportive of the working mom Jamie. However, thirty months later, she has proven herself to her company (and appointed VP!) and her whole family. Happy mom, Happy life. Finally, her searching and her struggles have been rewarded. And yours can be, too.

Become the Lead in Your Elevator Pitch

You have to become your own champion and cheerleader and grab the attention of busy people. Now you have to sell yourself with a sound bite.

Enter the elevator pitch: a brief, persuasive speech that you use to spark interest without sounding like you're reading from a cue card. Your spiel should be clear and memorable, and last no longer than a short *elevator* ride of sixty seconds. A minute of validation: I know it's hard to self-promote when you are feeling down and unemployed, and for sure there is shame associated with not working, which can be demoralizing, even debilitating. However, after weeks of searching for and boosting your confidence, it's time to walk tall, stand proud, and go for it. Once you get it right, it will be empowering to create a flattering, concise elevator pitch, a well-practiced career rap you can comfortably relay during cocktail party conversation, as well as a job interview.

A Nonworking Mom

Often the at-home mom helicopters all her energy into boosting her kid's success by repeating

"You is kind, you is smart, you is important."
—Aibileen Clark, *The Help*

Great for the kids, but you need to helicopter your own success too. Find your own self-advocating and comforting mantra. Own it . . . then press

REFRESH.

REFRESH.

REFRESH.

Imagine you randomly bump into a college friend at the airport or an ex-colleague at a school event. After exchanging pleasantries, you're asked the devil question: *What are you up to these days?* You open your mouth and—nothing. Today, let's prepare a ready-to-go Elevator Pitch, so that you can grab it out of your pocket whenever or where ever needed.

How Did SHE Do It?
She chose hard work and the high road and prevailed.

Brooke M., executive coach and networking advisor, mother of two, cancer survivor

Brooke was the spunky child of California sunshine and never questioned her dad's encouraging refrain that "nothing's impossible." All she ever wanted to be was an executive.

Her first job out of college was a 100% commission salesperson for Xerox. And by age twenty-five, she had won back a $1-million contract for Xerox. Bravo. She had two daughters, and for the next fifteen years, she kept getting promoted within the Xerox Corp. Her "nothing's impossible" bandwagon kept playing her tune. Then, in her mid-thirties, Brooke turned down a promotion that would require her family to relocate to headquarters in Upstate New York. Brooke's was a no-fault exit story; she had hit the Xerox glass ceiling for Southern California.

She took a break, enjoyed mothering, and then reloaded her career as an executive for a local scientific medical company. Onward as a triple threat: she was an upbeat salesperson, she could be succinct and authoritative, and she thrived under pressure in a corporate boardroom.

Then she got a dire breast cancer diagnosis and summoned every morsel of her grit and grace to, somehow, beat her odds. During her long rides to and from treatments, she had plenty of time to soul-search, and she became certain of her perfect calling: a professional corporate coach. With freshly shorn hair from her chemo, Brooke traveled to Hudson Institute in Santa Barbara and became a certified executive coach.

And now, she's a freelance life coach consultant to major corporations. When a valued executive is struggling through a professional bump or a trauma, their company calls in Brooke to sustain positive change. All the skills that Brooke had mastered over the years as a veteran executive blended with her no-nonsense style of parenting, and her serious brush with mortality made her an excellent and certified expert on strategic supervising, effective elevator pitching, maximizing resources, and coaching executives to be their very best. Brooke had many career experiences, each that suited her at different moments as her life changed. She ducked. She dove. She soared.

The "what do you do?" question.

You never know who you may run into walking the dog, when you're in line at the movie theater, or at a doctor's office building lobby. Always have your ice-breaking and branded pitch ready-to-go so you can quickly turn an awkward conversation into a casual pitching opportunity.

> *"Always keep your nicest robe in your grabs reach*
> *. . . you never know when there is going to be a fire in the*
> *middle of the night and. . . . you never know*
> *who else will be out on the street."*
> —Grandmother Sophie, Fall River, Massachusetts

Elevator Pitch Advice from the Corporate Executive Guru

• Keep it simple:	2 to 4 sentences; 60 to 90 seconds.
• Practice:	Stand tall, and project a warm presence.
• Know your audience:	Look them in the eye.
• Be direct:	"I market a product for people who want X."
• Be specific:	"I like to help people who are disabled."
• Be welcoming so the listener will say:	"Tell me more about that."
• Help people help you:	"I am looking for a position in a firm that does X."
• Ask for what you want:	"Can you introduce me to Mr. X in that field?"

In the last hour, you nailed down your job targets. Don't get shy now, my friend. I know that for some, selling might be just as hard as asking, but if your talking points are solid, and you've practiced and repeated it enough times and with pride, you've got this.

Sounds simple enough, right? But condensing decades of a life into a 60-second compelling statement that packs a punch can feel as challenging as threading a needle without your reading glasses. Here's a little help.

Reach-In Exercise: PRODUCE YOUR PITCH.

Start by picking one hypothetical meet-up. Imagine you randomly run into a mom from Teddy's Tot playgroup that you haven't seen in years. She now works in property management for a prominent real estate firm. Two kids. Husband is a lawyer. A pretty nonthreatening acquaintance. After a decade apart, how do you describe yourself? Begin to specifically announce your ideal job quest, and make sure it includes:

- Previously, I . . . and just getting back now.
- A concise and proud goal: "I want to be a . . ."
- A rationale why this goal is a positive match. "I'm excited because I've always gravitated towards . . ."
- Don't brag, but don't hide your strengths, either. Humbly share your best qualities.
- Don't forget to make this pitch a conversation, and include a question back to your acquaintance. Be natural. Be yourself. Don't sound rehearsed (even though you will be!).
- Ask the other person what they're up to.

Sample Elevator Pitch: 65 Seconds of "You" Speak

"I've decided to go back to work . . . it's time. I used to work full-time for an architect and fell in love with interior design—which I relied on when we rebuilt our fixer-upper. I've mastered giving homes a facelift on a tight budget, I can guess the outcome of every home-makeover reality show, and have been helping out friends for practice. I love decorating and just got a part-time job restaging properties for open houses. My ex-boss (drop their name) knows a ton of designers and has asked for a portfolio, so I believe they can recommend me to clients. I'd love to show you my portfolio, too . . . I would love your opinion."

Next, refer back to your Fave Five from yesterday and imagine yourself stuck in an elevator for 60–90 seconds with the person you want to employ you. You are on. Channel your inner Melanie Griffith (who was in an elevator!) as Tess in "Working Girl" when the big boss asks her to describe how she came up with the idea to sell him on a radio station.

Your elevator pitch is launched. Now you can keep evolving and perfecting it. Proudly wear your pitch out in public as often as possible. Rehearse it in front of the mirror. If you are really brave, you can record a video of your pitch on your smart phone . . . anything to practice, practice, practice. Eventually, you will have secured your confidence enough to go out into the world. Practice with the flight attendant on a long flight home, or accept an invite to a former colleague's event. I promise, the more clearly you sell yourself, the more attractive you become as a hire when the rubber hits the road and you're interviewing in real life.

Public speaking is a muscle that needs active use to get strong. For example, I can usually express myself quite well on paper, but I am in awe of people who can stand on a stage and give a speech or roll out a toast without a script. Many powerful people short-circuit in front of crowds or get tongue-tied when called upon to present a point or make a toast.

Being ambitious is your birthright. You are entitled to a career you love. Never apologize for being assertive, for wanting praise, for taking charge, or for getting credit for a job well done. Claiming credit for your own good deeds and being able to sell yourself is something that gets easier with practice. You need to get out of your domestic bubble and speak up, again and again. Lawyers do it. Teachers do it. Remember as a child how much you loved to hear your voice magnified through an annoying microphone? Push yourself into karaoke mode. And if you practice, you will incrementally improve, and eventually command a room.

If it's a real push for you to get out there and sell yourself, check your local colleges for extension courses in public speaking and sign up for one.

DEB TELLS ALL

For me, when asked, "So what are you doing these days?" my elevator pitch goes like this:

"Well, I am finishing a book, due out in January . . . it's an upbeat guide for capable moms who want to go back to work and are a little bewildered how to get back in. The book is designed like a chic recipe book with simple steps geared toward moms. Nope . . . I'd never written a book before, I'd read plenty and always loved being a strategic and a bossy girlfriend. I knew there was an audience because I spent many afternoons waiting right behind these moms in the carpool lane. So I researched and leaned on my networks, created a series of exercises and work prompts, and—in between other jobs—I wrote . . . and wrote. I got ignored and rejected a lot . . . until finally a friend of a friend introduced me to an agent, and a publisher took a chance. And now **Moms for Hire: 8 Steps to Kickstart Your Next Career** *is going to be published as a "resolution book." Most moms seem to love talking about this work/life dilemma. At any given time there are five and a half million stay-at-home moms with kids under fifteen years old . . . just look around this room* (always a quick pause here) *. . . see, all deserving moms who took time off, and whose talent and hidden ambitions are probably stalled. So many of them need this book . . . hopefully they will pick it up and find their professional mojo . . . How did you figure your path?"*

Lucky for me, I found a group of folks and a cause I really cared about, and so it's easy to "put it out there" with conviction and confidence. And that passion has carried me through the years of inexperience, wrong turns, and long hauls. I believe I have tapped into a sisterhood of most moms, all of whom feel some some guilt and some regret . . . and a lot of pride, too. I'd know when I have given a good elevator pitch because the pitchee would chime in, engaged in telling their own (or their sister's or mother's) story . . . And then once you have hooked the listener, they might offer a suggestion about how I might be able to sell the book, or who might help with a blurb.

Alternative Fun Inspiration

If you are still stuck creating your elevator pitch or you are uncomfortable delivering your pitch, pause and amuse yourself with a few elevator riffs on Youtube. It's valuable to witness others going through the same struggle and taking command of their pitch.

Party Tricks for the Shy Girl

A few party tricks for the shy girl that lives inside of you:

- When asking for a favor, *imagine you are soliciting for someone else*—especially if it's for a kid's need.
- It's always more empowering to advocate for a cause rather than for yourself.
- *Watch others* who are comfortable with public speaking (talks show hosts, lecturers, yoga instructors, etc.). You will discover their common denominator is that they are all excellent listeners.
- *Know your audience*. Every crowd is different. Assess your audience and speak to them.
- *Pick a focal person*. Breathe, relax, and direct your words to the best version of that single supportive face.
- *Practice* in front of a mirror, or into a microphone, and play it back. You might find that you do a great job after all!
- Most of your discomfort stems from being uncomfortable with how you *believe* you present. Get over that. And spit out your gum.
- *Write down and even memorize* your pitch.

" *The way you overcome shyness is to become so wrapped up in something that you forget to be afraid.* "
—Lady Bird Johnson

Also, you could tune into an episode of Shark Tank and take notes. Watch how real amateurs pitch their sauces and steamers. Sure, those jolly hucksters are coached before they are thrown up onto national television, but still, in a very short window these everyday people connect to their audience, display their product, and hopefully co-opt you into their future. Hey, if they can pitch-it, so can you.

Reach-Out Exercise: GO SHOPPING! BUT FIRST, FLUSH OUT THE OLD.

You will probably need to update your look. Even if you have a fabulous wardrobe, there is something inspiring about getting yourself something new as you step into a new work world. Before you do any shopping, though, you'll want to get rid of at least something in your closet. Make sure you're not holding onto any last remnants of eighties suits or nineties casual workday outfits. Flush that out. Then . . . shop!

Don't just buy another pair of yoga leggings. Dress and shop for the job you want to get. Go to the suit department if that's what you're going to need. Or buy a new pair of Crocs if you want to go back into hospital work. Take a friend. Try stuff on. Be purposeful. You need to present yourself as new and refreshed.

If your closet is up-to-date and plentiful, update your hairstyle or choose a new color nail polish. Buy a pair of shoes, a purse . . . something. Put it in your spending plan, and either save up for it or head out to the mall now.

Daily Do List

❏ Devised and practiced an elevator pitch.

❏ Signed up for a public speaking workshop.

❏ Sent three friend requests for potential contacts.

❏ Shopped for clothes or changed to non-mom haircut.

Write a Spirited Cover Letter Template

Don't blow off the cover letter. Trust me. A compelling cover letter can make the difference between which pile your application is dropped into: the "meh" or the "yeah!" And yes, you need to hit a few key beats in that letter. But the most important factor in this letter is that it is clearly written and a quick read. The infamous Elle Woods of *Legally Blonde* printed her perfumed résumé on pink paper; others might send along a memorable treat or toy. There is a chance of overkill backfiring on you, but if you have a mark of distinction that fits your personality, by all means, personalize your cover letter and résumé. Just keep it short, to the point, and pithy.

Beyond the clever attention getter, there are a few musts for a successful cover letter. Make sure you cover the basics and then sprinkle in a little personality.

Cover Letter Musts:

Address your cover letter to a real person with a heartbeat.

Find the name of a specific recruiter, the hiring manager, the head of human resources. Also, if you want to be in a specific department in the organization, and if you know the name of a person in a specific department, write to them directly. However, you should cover your bases and always send along a copy of your résumé and the cover letter to the human resources department.

Paragraph # 1—Praise Them and Introduce Yourself

Compliment their company and introduce your intentions to want to work there. Also, clearly state the job position you are interested in. If you're being referred by someone, mention their name in this opening paragraph. If you wish, you could add where you discovered the job opening and the office location where you'd like to work.

Paragraph #2—Show Off Your Stuff

Prove that you're attractive. Showcase your knowledge of the company and how you are right for the position. Without repeating your résumé, state one direct experience or one anecdote that shows your talent and how you would fit in. Use their job description to outline how you meet their specific job requirements. This should be one paragraph that ties in your understanding of their company, and, most important, the job position and your ability to do it well.

Paragraph #3—Thank Them and Suggest a Next Step
Thank them, and repeat how you would like to join their team. Make it clear that you want to make their job easier, and that you will follow up within a week to make sure your application is in order; directly let them know you would love to meet them and will call next week to set up an interview. Over and out.

Check and double-check for typos, spelling, and grammatical errors. You don't want them to think they are hiring a sloppy person.

Work hard on this cover letter. Give it some zest and personality. The hope is that with a little tinkering and a new address, you will be able to send the same engaging cover letter out to all the thirty to fifty employers you're scouting.

What Every Future Boss or Recruiter Wants to Hear from a *Mom for Hire.*
What is the boss looking for? What makes you an attractive candidate?
By now, you know what will help you become an expert in your job arena. Now it's time to actualize your fantasy. You've narrowed down your prospects to the spots where you could excel with passion. Let's find the best path to storm the kingdom and show off your confidence and charm.

All employers are looking for five essential qualifications from a job hunter. They want to be certain that:

1. You want to be an *active part* of their fabulous company and you will make their life easier.
2. You *fill their needs* and will not become *a need* yourself. You bring them solutions, not problems.
3. You are *a good team player* and will mesh into their company brand.
4. You are "*better*" *than the competition.*
5. They *can afford you!* You want to show you are in each other's league; you are a match and a catch. As in dating, both parties want to think they are getting a good deal—an enthusiastic, capable woman who will enhance their business. Prepare and tuck away couple personal anecdotes or fitting references that sideways prove you are both a "match" and a "catch."

You've worked hard to clarify your cravings and build your confidence. You've made peace with your past and are perched to propel yourself into the job-of-your-choice. Now it's time to send and submit your résumé to at least twenty places, and soon begin to interview.

Daily Do List

❏ Wrote my cover letter template.

❏ Finished one version of my résumé.

❏ Double-checked my letter and résumé for typos, etc.

❏ Begged an expert or a Core Four friend to proofread my pages.

Hour Five
Apply, Apply, Apply!

So far, in this step you have named your specific job targets and found the names and addresses for the actual job that will match your passions, your profile, and your reality. You have created a dashing résumé and a spirited cover letter. And now, with pride, you will culminate your weeks of work by applying for a job! Can you believe it?! Amazing.

> *"Getting hired is a marathon not a sprint."*
> —Fran Helms, Recruiting Executive

Press Send: Apply to Your Top Tier Today.

Get the letters and résumés out to your Fave Five first, keeping in mind a Plan B. For every job-of-interest for which you apply, keep your eyes and heart open—many similar (perhaps not as obviously branded) jobs are out there, and one might be just right for you. For every Plan A, cover-lettered résumé you send out, you need to expand your reach and be prepared to submit to similar companies that are not your Fave Five. Also, every time you meet or talk to someone in your field-of-interest—even if they don't have a job opening—ask them if they know someone else you could talk to. *Job contacts beget job contacts . . .beget JOBS.* This is the time to get fearless and tireless. Apply and apply and apply and apply. And apply.

- List your *Fave Five*.
- Look on their website to see if any specific jobs are being offered within that company. If not:
  - Send a cold cover letter to their HR department.
  - Find a point-person who works at that company and send a cover letter and résumé to that specific person, too.
- Scour your friends list and ask if they know anybody who knows anybody.

As you begin applying, keep a thorough log of when and who you reached out to. (Application Tracker inserted and on my website.) By the subsequent week, you will be following up on those letters and applications and making every effort to set up an interview or a swing-by for an informational meeting as soon as possible.

Application Tracker				
Date Applied	Company/Position	In-House Contact	Feedback/Next Step	Time to Nudge

Additional Application Tracker pages are available to download at DeborahJelinNewmyer.com

Daily Do List

❑ Finalize my résumé. Polish my charming cover letter.

❑ CREATE a Plan B.

❑ APPLY. APPLY. APPLY.

❑ Begin my Application Log.

Step Six
GETTING TO THE INTERVIEW

"Winners don't quit and quitters don't win."
— Yifat Oren, event planner, maven, mother of two

Hour Goals

Hour One:	Rise above your insecurities and don't give up.
Hour Two:	Prep for your interviews.
Hour Three:	Travel down the noncorporate/non-HR avenues.
Hour Four:	Charmingly stalk your contacts & find an interview outfit.
Hour Five:	Ace the interview!

This week, you will turn your job-hunting into a determined and consistent habit. Over the next five days, your goal is to set up and prepare for as many interviews as possible. You've sent out your original feelers to your Fave Five job spots. Fantastic. Now you need to follow up with all these newfound prospects.

Remember to use the application log with everyone you reached out to. If you are more computer-nimble, you are welcome to set up a tracker in Excel, or wherever your keyboard comfort takes you. Like that polite pause after a first date, give them 3 or 4 days to respond before you feel rejected. Then reach back out to them, trying your best to schedule an interview. I find the second and third follow-up calls to be the most challenging. Sure, rejection might be looming, but being active, determined and politely nudging can distinguish you from a pool of other qualified applicants.

Don't Let Fear Take You Down.

It's a waste to fear rejection. You are going to be rejected. You are going to be ignored. Sometimes that rejection can have a cause, and it is worth tracking down the reason for the pass. However, sometimes the rejection is completely random and totally out of your control.

Remember that once you become an asker, the worst thing that can happen is that you get a *no*. And a no is free and cannot actually hurt you. Still, always ask, and pay no mind if you are initially turned down; you only need one yes.

Advocate for Yourself. Again. And Again.

So sorry, but over these next couple of weeks you will lose control over the time clock. You can do your best to become the employer's urgent priority, but honestly, the ball is in their court, and it can be tricky to rush a response. After all these weeks of step-by-step determined work on your part, you now have to just become a polite "waiter." Waiting can be challenging and ego-deflating. Waiting for a call back. Waiting for an interview. Waiting for an email response. Please know that being ignored is not the same as being rejected. Rarely does the hirer feel your sense of urgency. Sorry again, but corporate time is not like personal time. What feels like a month of your letter sitting on someone's desk may only feel like days to the person being asked to read it.

Again, another needle to be threaded: you are still interested and still interesting. You need to follow up with charm and be proactive in this job quest without crossing the line to stalking.

After One Week:

Rookie mistake: After one week of real time, if you haven't heard back, double-check that you applied to the correct address and the email address was exact. Way too obvious, but also way too common . . . Open your "Sent" folder and make triple-sure you added that "m" to the ".com" . . . and that the email didn't get misfiled with your "Drafts."

Spam Alert: If you haven't heard back from anyone within one week of submitting, there is a solid chance your email went directly to a spam file. Spam is especially sensitive to any unknown email when it arrives with an attachment. With that in mind, resending that same email will also get forwarded onto the company's spam mail. Also, many organizations add on a spam filter just to weed out unsolicited requests. Once you've waited a week from the day you initially submitted your résumé, call the office. You can use the excuse of wanting to confirm that they received your letter, and then use that opening to get friendly and follow up.

<u>*Follow Up with Intel*</u>: Look for a article, a notice, or any new information that refers to some detail of your interview. Use that tinder of news to fuel a reminder to the employer that you're on top of things.

<u>*Find a Mole*</u>: If you know anybody who knows the employer, or has any inside information . . . call them and ask for insight as to how long you might have to wait to hear back. If the hiring manager or targeted boss has a friendly assistant or the company has a welcoming receptionist, reach out. No contact is too small.

<u>*Call the Assistant:*</u> As politely as possible, see if they have had a chance to review. Today's assistant could be tomorrow's vice president.

No Shame in Your Game . . . Embrace Your Second Tier
Five, even ten sends are not enough!

This step will motivate you to reach beyond the borders of your ideal job. You have found the jobs that fit your passions, your profile, and your reality. You have applied to specific jobs, HR departments, and targeted workers. And now, for every ideal job you have uncovered, you need to pursue as many similar (perhaps not-as-seemingly-perfect) jobs.

If your ideal job is to work designing shoes for Tom's One-for-One, and they aren't currently hiring, maybe you can get your foot in the door at this great company by doing the following:

- Apply for a job as a receptionist or in customer service.
- Apply for a temporary position, even if it's as an intern or floater.
- Take that part-time job at a local shoe store to gain shoe cred.
- Help out your friend at her fabric store. It's retail, but she also needs designing and organizing assistance.
- Keep following up with HR. They are always busy and someone is always flaky.
- Keep looking for anyone who might know anyone at your Fave company.

 DEB TELLS ALL

"Not a chance."
"Not going to happen."
"It's a pass."
"You're spinning your wheels."
"Give it up . . . Move on."

We've all had these bummer bombs dropped upon our head. From powers-that-be, from our own negative turntable, and even from friends being "supportive." Banish these echoing bummer beats. Do everything you can to be emboldened by defeat. Even though it looks like you have hit a wall, keep traveling. Push through the skip of that broken record of doubts and defeats.

All and all, I have had a very fortunate career. I competed and succeeded in a rough industry for years and mostly, I have enjoyed a relatively secure and stimulating career. Sure, I worked hard, but I was also extremely lucky to balance life and work and love. And yet, I was no longer performing at my best. At some point, either my job or my husband or my kids or my waistline got ignored. But I kept my head up and rolled with the good and the bad. I probably wasted energy comparing myself to other successes. Too often, I felt underachieved. But always always always . . . I refused to give up. I had to summon a lot of discipline (and denial) to turn off numerous defeats.

After my husband passed away, I was amazingly given a small housekeeping deal by a true friend at Sony Pictures Entertainment. We all knew it was partially a pity deal from my generous friends; I was a struggling widow of four needy kids. However, I also had some talent and connections and a smart nose for material, and I was determined to activate it all and earn my supper. My streamlined and scrappy team was given a lovely office on the Sony Lot in Culver City, and we tirelessly went about scouting and packaging films.

One project that consumed me was a modern college movie about an a cappella group, which we had titled *Don't Stop Believing*. I could not carry a tune, nor was I great at remembering lyrics, but I had a vision for a modern college movie that could become a classic. During every visit to schools with my oldest daughter, the backward-walking tour guide would brag about the number of a cappella groups on their campus. News to me. As the Greek houses were waning at many colleges and universities, singing groups were rising up to fill the social vacuum. These pun-filled names—The Harmonics; The Aca-belles; the Vocal-tronics—were offering young coeds a niche of identity, and a place to gather and to belong. Surpisingly, a cappella was becoming hip.

I pitched and pitched and convinced Sony to invest in a script; but the writer, director, and producer were all over fifty years old, and the studio doubted we were cool enough to capture a young, movie-going crowd. We tried everything to prove we were *au courant* and that there would be an audience for college kids spontaneously breaking out in pop songs. We even considered changing the names on the script to our millennial children so the screenplay would have a more contemporary flair. In fairness, our timing was a bit early and we were pushing harmonic singing groups before *GLEE* and *The Voice* hit big, and on-screen singing still seemed "uncool." It happens. It wasn't personal and no fault assigned. Our team wasn't able to rally enough "x-factor" to push the Sony brass into making our college a cappella movie. That broken record again of "Never gonna happen . . . give it up . . . not here . . ." kept playing on repeat.

Instead, and perhaps to get me off their back, the head of the studio suggested that we try to turn a cappella into a reality TV show. So I crossed the lot and took a meeting of Sony Alternative Television, which was just ramping up. Luckily, Holly Jacobs and I liked each other. In our first meeting, we bonded over our daughters, who had happened to go to the same high school. And Holly had helped out with a volunteer project I had initiated at our daughter's school. So job-hunters, remember to keep active and connected even if it isn't always producing a paycheck. You never know when a volunteering gig will have a karmic boomerang.

Also, I had come recommended by the Sony Feature division, and she was politely curious. In another stroke of luck, Holly's only daughter was in a high school madrigal group, and Holly had witnessed the power of teenagers *singing in harmony*. Honestly, she was only guardedly interested. Still, she offered us a bit of development money to support us to see how we could develop a pitching tool, called a sizzle reel. We went to an a cappella competition . . . we filmed a few local college groups . . . and we borrowed from the Internet to put together a *sizzling* three-minute commercial pitch that showed off our a cappella concept. It was raw and shoestring, but we were also able to display harmonic group singing as sexy and aspirational on campus life. At Cornell. At Duke. At NYU. At UCLA. Real images of excited coeds in short tops . . . adorable geeks . . . ironically preppy quartets . . . soulful street singers. Definitely a vibrant collection of YouTube watchable reality. Our sizzle reel became an easy promotional link to fund. We took it out to all the buyers (networks and cable) who would partner with Sony and put our little show on the air. And then, that blasted echo came back again: *"Not for us . . . It's a pass . . . Give it up."*

I remember heading back from the Culver City car wash, and in a clean car and good mood, when Holly called me to formally pass. Huh? Nooooooooooo . . . and so instead of politely accepting the "pass," I barreled onward, pretending like I did not hear her "pass." Holly had earnestly tried to sell our show, but for some reason, nobody got it, and she was at the end of pushing this a cappella string uphill. Somehow, I kept talking, and I convinced her of the "10 percent further" rule. So, she took one more shot and gave a pitch to Live TV director Joel Gallen, who had some recent success with the *Rock n Roll Hall of Fame* and *America's Best Dance Crew*. Eureka. He loved the sizzle, and the networks wanted Joel. With Joel, we got the meetings . . . and the pieces fell into place. NBC offered us four two-hour event shows around the holidays, and *The Sing-Off* was born and went on to air for NBC for five seasons. We got better and better. We dealt with internal squabbles and network complaints, and finally we rated enough to keep going. In season three, The Grammy-winning group Pentatonix was born . . . and a cappella reached a mainstream pitch. Another studio smartly launched *Pitch Perfect,* and a cappella is now legitimately beloved. Our little engine that could, did.

I had never had been rejected so many times. I had never made a television show before. Yet I kept on visualizing the best version on **The Sing-Off,** and I kept on believing. I became notorious as the producer who could not hear "It's a pass." I believed there was always another way around the gatekeeper. Another strategic way to get to a yes. Warning: During the next few weeks, maybe months, those sirens of defeat might be singing in your ears. Take a deep breath and keep going. Ten percent further. Always ten percent further.

> "*It reminds me of that old joke—you know, a guy walks into a psychiatrist's office and says, 'Hey doc, my brother's crazy! He thinks he's a chicken.' Then the doc says, 'Why don't you turn him in?' Then the guy says, 'I would but I need the eggs.'*"
> —Woody Allen

Reach-Out Exercise: LOOK BEYOND THE NAME BRAND . . . SOMETIMES IT'S EVEN A BETTER FIT.

While you are actively pursuing your Fave Five dream companies, make sure you also are looking at the less obvious, less prestigious employer you could also be happy working for. College counselors call the "Ivies" most students' *stretch* schools, but don't forget to also find a *safety* college. And try to find a *safety* that will still feel like a win. For every Google, McCann Erickson, Marvel Comics, or Annie Leibovitz you want to work for, there are probably ten other upstart versions of your ideal job. Search for tomorrow's independent production company, start-up tech, local ad agency, or the gift shop two towns over.

As in yoga class, we are shown a pose and then given permission to *modify the pose.* For every job-of-interest you apply to, keep your eyes and heart open to opportunity. For every cover-lettered résumé you send out, send out ten more to a facsimile version of that job. Every time you meet or talk to someone in your field-of-interest, even if they don't have a job opening, ask them if you know someone else you could talk to. Jobs beget jobs. Now is not the time to get tired or shy. As long as you remain organized and open, and keep good track of your applications and your allies, you can never overapply.

> "If you have been on the job search for a while, **you're not alone**. About 40 percent of the nearly 13.3 million unemployed Americans have been without a job for six months, according to the Bureau of Labor Statistics. Additionally, of that 40 percent, four million have been jobless for a year or more. On top of that, it takes the average American job seeker about 39 weeks to find a job after being released."
>
> Alan Carniol, *Interview for Success*

Now that you have shined a spotlight on your arena of interest, you need to become a detective in your desired marketplace. If you have moved up the ladder in banking, but you really want to be a writer, find out which copywriting, essay tutoring, magazine receptionist, travel journal jobs, etc., are offered that exist in the real world. Grab your net and cast it out widely.

This is not about lowering your standards; instead, rephrase your broadening search and call it *expanding your outreach*. Sometimes, settling is a godsend. This hour you'll throw several hats in the ring, even if it wasn't your dream ring. Look for alternative companies to the brand version you originally hunted. Seek out the "8s," not just the "10s."

Try the younger, smaller, maybe further away option. That brand name today might not be "all that" tomorrow. Figure out which other companies are doing work similar to the company you favor. You might actually find them to be a better match.

There is a job for you. It might not immediately be for the exact company you want, but it could be a stepping-stone to more than you ever imagined.

And if you absolutely have to work at Bloomingdale's and Macy's just won't do, march into Bloomingdales' HR and tell them you will do anything for them, even if it's not on the floor. You might have to work in the basement luggage department instead of the first floor Prada section, but you're willing to do whatever you have to for the company. If you are only offered work as a temp, or for a lesser salary, or as a front line greeter, think twice before you turn down any foot-in-the-door job.

To Mail or to Email—Always a Question

It's the 21st century and the Job Fortresses have gone cyber, but don't totally give up on endangered fifty-cent snail mail. Yet. Most corporate, government, and large nonprofit jobs ONLY accept applications and résumés on-line. Often, HR is outsourced to other groups,

How Did SHE Do It?
Mother Bear channeled her fury into a business.
Celia T., mother of four, painter-turned-small business owner, Oceanside, California

Celia's childhood had been nomadic: her family moved twelve times before she was seventeen and only ever allowed two suitcases per move. When she married and had four children within five years, she promised herself no one would ever be told "pack your bags . . . we're moving." Instead, she fiercely created a stable home that became the go-to hub of the neighborhood. Their driveway was bustling with a constant pick-up game, and she always welcomed an extra mouth around the solid oak dinner table. Celia kept herself content and busy with every detail that would make her family feel secure and settled in their home.

As her children grew, they each found extracurricular passions: one a focused club soccer goalie, another a noisy electric guitarist, and the twins fell in love with crew racing. In California, rowing is becoming a serious sport, but in Celia's area there was really only one coach and one club team. Her youngest were twins, and thus, naturals in tandem play. But they were slender and not outwardly muscular. And the town's only crew coach turned out to be mean and was quickly dismissive of Celia's kids. This triggered Celia's mother bear instinct into action. Like the heroine in a Lifetime movie, Celia gathered all the smaller, crew-interested kids and started her own team. It took a lot of political and administrative maneuvering, but with a gutsy strategic focus, Celia rented the boats, equipment, and facility time from the City Marina. She raised money, hired another coach; bought insurance and broadened her social outreach with Facebook and Instagram. She launched a second crew team with all the rejected kids from her area. It was rough seas to begin with, and the original coach became even meaner. But her kids and their team are thriving, and they have begun winning.

Also, Celia was always paying attention from the sidelines of her older son's club soccer team, and she co-opted a few of their time-tested routines for the new crew team. She began to divide the team tasks, monetized the events, and created fun gear. And now a junior-feeder team has been formed, and a few surrounding towns are following Celia's blueprint and starting-up crew teams, too. By next crew season, the South Coast League will have expanded by five more teams. Inspired by her kid's passion, and sensing a gap and a need, Celia channeled her frustrations and invented a new business. A salty cheer to Celia; she set an empowered example both to her kids and other capable moms.

and the application process can become very rigid and depersonalized. In fact, it often requires superior detective sleuthing to find the hard address of many companies. Online applying can be a convenience to some but statistically not the best way to land a dream job. Even if the application is of the on-line variety, I would suggest that you make the extra effort to also snail-mail in your application. Even try to make a personal visit to the office site. You might never get past the security gate or the receptionist, but an eye-to-eye effort is commendable and might win you points.

Many times you need to play the online route to get your foot into the company's hiring system. However, assuming that your are capable, the offer scale will be tipped based on personal interactions and your connections. The online fortress is here to stay. Become comfortable with all things cyber . . . enjoy its convenience and speed . . . but do not forget to make as many face-to-face appearances as possible. The impact of your human effort and energy will always be better than any avatar.

Homework Cheat Sheet:

LinkedIn: An absolute imperative. If you join only one site, LinkedIn covers all things. It's the biggest and the most comprehensive. It's got all aspects of the job hunt covered.

Apresgroup.com: An upscale site dedicated to women reentering the workforce. Very classy and sleek website. Definitely worth joining for its advice and readability. Its hiring database is growing nationally and already is plugged in to many fabulous urban opportunities.

Glassdoor.com: This website is the Yelp of companies from an employee and interviewee perspective. Great for the search and decision phase.

Craigslist.com: So easy. So prevalent. Always worth a quick peek.

ZipRecruiter.com: This site allows you to specify criteria and lets you see the progress of your application. While most sites feel like a one-way black hole . . . ZipRecruiter lets you know when your résumé has been opened. It also has a 1-click apply feature that lets you apply to jobs quickly without necessarily needing to write a new cover letter.

TheMuse.com: Good for finding start-ups and innovative companies, it also has great articles for any modern job seeker.

Indeed.com: Good general website for all jobs all over the country, but it's very popular, so you need to keep up and act fast.

All these sites start off free . . . and then—often—offer you premium services for a fee. That seems fair to me; everyone should get paid for their work. I suggest poking around all these sites, and then pick one or two to delve into and perhaps join up for fuller coaching and advice.

Once you sign up for any of these sites, they will flood your inbox daily. This can be overwhelming and a major time suck. Once you subscribe, give the site a week or two, and if you are not actively using them and you are ignoring their emails, do not let them hoard your inbox. Unsubscribe. Again and always, clutter kills.

Also beware: many of the listings are often stale listings. Probably the company was required to list a job opening—either on their own website or publicly—but that particular job might have gone up internally weeks ago. And might be very close to being filled. Don't bother becoming frustrated by knocking on all those doors, that's the way the work world works. If you really feel like you must work at a specific company, breach their wall by accepting any offered position to get inside the sanctum.

Daily Do List

❏ PRESSED SEND to at least five new job possibilities that were facsimiles of my Fave Five.

❏ Applied to the company of my choice, but for a lesser position.

❏ Followed up with the companies I applied to last week.

❏ Fought off going bonkers by "mantra-ing" perks and gratitude.

❏ Kept up with my Application Tracker.

Hour Two . . . (and Beyond)
Prep for Your Interviews

You've spent the last week applying to various jobs with a single-minded goal to get yourself an interview. Your strategy is to set up as many interviews as possible, then to turn that interview into a second interview.

How to get the interview? Follow up. Follow up. Follow up.

By now you have thrown at least a dozen (or two) spitballs up against the job wall, and you've written them down in your application tracker. You've waited a few days—maybe even a week. It's time to call or email those contacts and ask to see them face-to-face. Remember, their neglect is not necessarily rejection.

And if for some reason the HR department or your person says the position is filled, try to get into the office for an informational meeting. It's helpful to get an insider's peek and try to set foot in as many office spaces as you can. Things have changed in the marketplace, and a first hand look can give you a vital edge. Personally, I like to touch the fabric of a sweater, test out the smartphone before I commit, and tour colleges before my child applies. . . . Likewise, a face-to-face meeting always creates the best outcome.

Interview Prep

I polled many HR experts and job recruiters to discover the most frequently asked questions. They are usually pretty general and straightforward. The biggest feat will be to pepper your interview with confidence without sounding like a show-off. Be comfortable within your skin, and look the interviewer in the eye. And most important, enjoy yourself. Before the interview, look over this list of sample questions, and feel okay answering them with ease:

- Always start off with a compliment about the company and express your knowledge of their mission, vision, purpose, etc., and always express gratitude for the interview.
- Listen to your interviewer. Do not interrupt. And respond with less than two-minute answers.
- Do your best to create a conversational atmosphere, but make sure you are prepared for any of the following trigger questions.

For me, the best way to practice for an interview is to speak directly into a mirror, or my smartphone. Talk to your own image. Ask yourself every question you think you might be asked.

Reach-In Exercise: GO INTO YOUR BATHROOM AND PRETEND YOU ARE BEING INTERVIEWED.

- What makes this a *best job* for you right now?
- What makes you think you can do this job?
- What makes you qualified to work here?
- Why should I hire you?
- What motivated you to apply here specifically?
- What do you know about the company's values and mission?
- Where else have you applied? What do you think of our competition?
- Do you want my job?
- What motivates you? Teamwork? Money? Family? Independence?
- Are you available to work overtime? Travel?
- Where do you see yourself in five years? What's in your "Picture Frame"?
- What was the last great joke you heard? You told?
- What was the last teamwork activity you participated in? What was your function?
- What was the last problem you personally solved?
- What made you want to leave your job? How was the exit from your previous job? What did you like least about your last job? Quick pitch of your Exit Story.
- How do you take personal ownership of decisions, right or wrong?
- What's your greatest victory? Your most mortifying botch?
- How do you explain your gap in employment?

Think-On-Your-Feet Questions

Try to be loose enough to have fun with the interviewer. When I interview a prospective candidate, I always drum up a hypothetical problem involving something I am currently working on so I can throw the interviewee right into the middle of one of my spur-of-the-moment problems and test how they might think on their feet. This also helps me gauge how much the interviewee knows about the tasks they'd be responsible for. Remember, the boss essentially wants to make sure you will make their life easier; will fit in; will be a good deal.

Prepare yourself to answer a few hypothetical problems that require resolution. Under the umbrella of my work environment, it might look like this:

- A screenplay I bought needs a better ending.
- An agent just lied to me; what should I do?
- How I could get *Hamilton* tickets.
- A reality show I am pitching needs to attach a host . . . Who do you like?

In researching and writing *Moms for Hire*, I read every book and article on women and careers I could get my hands on. I joined many self-help programs and became a rabid tester of every online job-seeking site: Personality Tests, the Monsters, and plenty of others. I put in my time to become an expert of the job-seeking marketplace. Many of these sites are good to fish around and may give you some insight or a proper push. The site that spoke directly to me, and was the easiest to navigate, and least quick to ask for payment was Alan Carniol's Interview for Success (http://www.interviewsuccessformula.com). He was a generous and smart advisor. And I found his strategies to be clever and very easy to implement. After months signing up for his advice, his Interview for Success is the only site I am still enjoying and still happy to read several times a week.

I also wanted to give a shout-out to a supersmart online interview launcher called HireArt. HireArt was cofounded by Elli Sharef, a Yale graduate with a passion to help job-seekers succeed. Sharef's thesis was that there are plenty of good—primarily entry-level—jobs, but there was a disconnect between the hirers and hires, so she created a tool that serviced both the "yin" looking for a job and the "yang" recruiting employers. Résumés and cover letters were not enough, as she noted that "job candidates often like to fluff up their experience, and sometimes they even outright lie about their abilities."

Other times, potentially great employees are overlooked because they have unorthodox backgrounds that don't match up with what an employer thinks they need in terms of experience. Sometimes these kinds of things are realized during the in-person interview. Unfortunately for many employers, they often don't discover how much a particular candidate may have oversold themselves until they've been hired and can't perform to expectations.

With its new applicant screening system, HireArt thinks it may have a solution: once you sign on to HireArt, you're prompted through a series of one-minute video interviews. The drill is that you can record and rerecord your answer as many times as you'd like until you are happy with your clip. From their website: "Instead of asking applicants to talk about their experience, HireArt has them actually perform a series of tasks. For example, if an interview candidate claims to be an expert in Excel, an employer on HireArt might ask them to create an Excel model using a dataset they provide, then have them upload the completed file. Another employer may instead want to hear a creative's pitch for a new product." Or if you want to try a job in sales or customer service, the HireArt model would let you exhibit your calm-under-duress ability, your ability to advocate for a production, and your behavior within a team.

Reach-Out Exercise: TAKE THE HIREART TEST:

Subscribe to HireArt.com and begin the process of applying for a job. Even if the actual job doesn't match your ideal picture frame. Signing up will help you practice the interviewing process. The more you prep for interviews, the more comfortable you will become. Inevitably, you will botch one of your first interview outings. So grab this great opportunity to practice.

Daily Do List

❑ Followed up on applications.

❑ Scheduled interview(s) in person or on Skype.

❑ Prepped for future interviews.

❑ Subscribed to interview-coaching website.

Hour Three
Attention: Freelancers. Academics. Entrepreneurs. Artists.

If you have no interest in the corporate realm and you're not feeling the Tahari suit, your application and résumé roads diverge somewhat here. You very much want to have a working career, but your personality, talent, or circumstances require different flexibilities and stylings. You have done your discovery, and you know the traditional job market is not your target.

Instead, your career path is leading you to be:

- An ENTREPRENUER
- A FAMILY BUSINESS Colleague
- An ARTIST
- A FREELANCE with a Talent
- A RETAIL saleswoman, manager, etc.
- A STUDENT

Even if your route might lead down different avenues, most of the previous exercises still apply to you: you still need to carve out your "ME" time, spotlight your specific and transferrable skills to reach back and cultivate your personal networks to clean up your personal glitches, and to keep going and going with renewed spunk and cheer.

While it's always helpful to have a résumé handy, if you're leaning away from company work, you may not need to focus on updating a résumé or cover letter. LinkedIn will always ask you for it, so might as well give it a try; they have plenty of networking potential for the less conventional job arenas. And if you are applying for alternative jobs, you will still need plenty of bragging tools. If you want to work for a Furniture Maker, a photo portfolio of your pieces would be better than a résumé. If you are starting your own dance studio, instead of a standard résumé, you might need to apply for a bank loan and make legal deals with landlords and partners. So you still will need to have all your stats and accomplishments in a tidy, brag-able package. You still need to be prepped for your interview and it's recommended that you leave behind some memorable token of your talent, craft, or skill. So even though there are plenty of career avenues where résumés *per se* are less essential, still a confident interview manner and *samples of your specialness* are extremely necessary.

How Did SHE Do It?
She turned her hobby into a jobby.

Sophia E., mother of two teenagers, happy wife, and now, an artist

Sophia was never a complainer. She'd grown up in a smart and supportive family that helped her overcome her learning dyslexia issues. Sophia was happy to play the likeable, pretty, albeit quieter, little sister role in a boisterous, very social family. She married an excellent man whom she loved and created a comfortable home for their two thriving children. All was good. As the tech world blossomed in Seattle, so too did the demands on her husband's legal expertise, and Sophia naturally drifted into the full-time parenting role. It was a traditional lifestyle, without questions or regrets. Yet after a decade of manning the home front, she began craving her own creative outlet. So Sophia began organizing her time and found the space to actualize all those images that had been swirling around in her head.

Sophia created seventeen cool collage art pieces. And suddenly, whatever zest motivated her to create this artistic series also amped up her personal confidence. And at age fifty, Sophia decided she could step out of her comfortable nest and expose herself as an artist. She noticed that her regular Seattle restaurant had lots of wall space. So she ASKED the server how they found their artists. A few phone calls and email exchanges later, the Sand Point Grill was exhibiting her images. She has already sold two pieces and has conjured up her next unique series idea. Now she can acknowledge herself as an artist on her passport. This was a new Sophia, and by example, she has inspired many of her mom pals to dig deep into their passion and make something happen. If SHE did it . . . so can they.

And as Sophia's self-confidence gelled, she became more energetic. Suddenly, she became aware of empty walls everywhere she turned. On every vacant space, Sophia saw a business opportunity. She retraced her own steps from being a garage artist to a paid professional, and she founded a company that curates the art in local restaurants and office buildings and matches these empty walls with emerging artists. It's a win/win for blank walls and previously unseen talent alike.

"A goal without a plan, is just a wish."
—Shonda Rhimes, Dartmouth Commencement Speech, May 2014

Entrepreneur vs. Employee

Not everyone is an entrepreneur. While you may love tuning into Shark Tank or even QVC to watch civilians sell their bright ideas to professional experts, not everyone has a great idea or invention. Not everyone wants to be risky. Not everyone wants to be the boss.

If you have an idea you're passionate about and want to march out and make that work, God love you. If you are not sure you have what it takes to go out on your own, I found this great evaluation that tests your mettle to become an entrepreneur. The questionnaire, found on LinkedIn, was written by big shot Peter Guber, movie mogul, CEO, and sports team owner.

Reach-In Exercise: ARE YOU AN ENTREPRENEUR?

Look down this list and push yourself through these questions. If they energize you, push on, Maverick. If they scare you into panic, maybe think again.

The Be-Your-Own-Boss Litmus Test	Let's Go	Nope
1. Can you clearly define and articulate your vision?	_____	_____
2. Can you give it a time limit so your vision becomes your goal?	_____	_____
3. Are you inspired by your vision or perspire at the thought of undertaking it?	_____	_____
4. Have you designed an entry plan for your product or process?	_____	_____
5. Can you clearly define who your audience/customers are?	_____	_____
6. Do you know your competition and the competitive landscape?	_____	_____
7. Are you able to differentiate your offering from your competitors?	_____	_____
8. Do you know what resources and resourcefulness you need to execute your plan?	_____	_____
9. Are you properly capitalized? If not, do you know where and how to seek sufficient capital to get liftoff for success?	_____	_____
10. Are you clear about what the treasures and time bombs of the journey might be?	_____	_____
11. Are you willing to not be risk-averse?	_____	_____

Continued . . .

12. Are you congruent? Do your feet, tongue, heart, and wallet go in the same direction?   _____   _____
13. Are you prepared to be reasonably uncomfortable with the uncertainty of "not knowing"?   _____   _____
14. Are you ready to be at the front of the parade?   _____   _____
15. Are you able to be the vision keeper, but be collaborative in the execution of your vision?   _____   _____
16. Can you keep your ego in check?   _____   _____
17. Are you able to bring in the best and brightest talent and motivate them?   _____   _____
18. Are you agile enough to take advantage of serendipity?   _____   _____
19. Are you able to manage success and be generous with the gold and glory?   _____   _____

Reach-Out Exercise: TEST OUT YOUR BRIGHT IDEA ON YOUR CORE FOUR.

If you're unsure whether going out on your own is the right path, ask your core four to take the Entrepreneurial Test on your behalf and trial pitch them your business plan.

Listen to and learn from their responses. If the results are clear and you're ready to take on entrepreneurship, take the next step. Be brave and smart as you chart your course to entrepreneurial success.

You might be an inventor with a brilliant idea, but you may not have the entrepreneurial skills and gut.

In that case, you need to find a partner who fills out that business quadrant you lack.

If you've got the desire (and the widget) to strike out on your own—there are many fantastic advice books and resources to be found. Bookstores and websites are overflowing with strategies for becoming an entrepreneur. It seems every successful entrepreneur has written a book.

And if you're looking to become inspired, pick up those best-selling memoirs from your favorite success stories. It seems that no rise to the top is complete without a published memoir of it. Dale Carnegie to Steve Jobs, Jeff Bezos to Suzie Orman, Tina Fey to Shonda Rhimes . . . they all have books!

Who inspires you? Pick your own personal hero. It's quite likely that they have a great tale to tell.

Joining the Family Business: Mom & Pop can be a Great Option

While job hunting can take a few months, occasionally jobs emerge out of a sudden lead: Your brother-in-law knows a dentist who needs front office help tomorrow. A cousin's catering business just lost their event planner. Your dad needs an in-house accountant he can trust. If you want to go back to work, and an opening pops up, be ready.

The greatest part of America's wealth lies with family-owned businesses.

- Family firms comprise 80 percent to 90 percent of all business enterprises in America.
- 78 percent of all new jobs are generated by family-owned businesses.
- *25 percent of family firms are helmed by women!*

DEB TELLS ALL

When my father was in his early thirties, just arriving home from World War II service in the Pacific arena, his dad lent him twelve thousand dollars to invest in a roofing cement factory in Clark, New Jersey. My dad worked hard and proudly grew Karnak Chemical into a successful manufacturing company. He was able to send his six kids to college and summer camp and continued to tithe to charity and take his wife on a nice vacation once a year. We never thought we were "rich," but we were always fed and clothed, and for the most part we all got along.

With three boys and three girls to choose from, my dad assumed one of us would carry on the family business. To date: four of the six kids worked in the office or the factory; when my Mom asked my sister, a practicing lawyer who was pregnant with her fourth child, to come by and help out on a specific legal matter, she felt capable to step in and lend advice. For her, the family business became a perfect nesting center for her legal skills and her personal interests. At first, she was able to work part-time as she learned the trade, and now, after nearly two decades of hard work and bumpy roads, Sarah Jane is president and has grown the business into four manufacturing facilities and six warehouses, nationwide, employing over eighty workers. And recently, the company has been certified as a Woman-Owned Business! Bravo to my sister's spectacular reinvention from a lawyer to a business and manufacturing maverick after age forty. In part, this is a story of right place at the right time. But also, her years and training as a lawyer and her mothering of four children were essential to her impressive job shift and success.

While a family-based business might not be your obvious dream job, nor does its product always fit your schooling or talent, a job offer with your family or through a family connection is a very common on-ramp. Think twice about turning down this inside edge.

Working with family (and/or friends) has pluses and minuses. If you leave your office and go straight from the boardroom to the dinner table, it is difficult to leave your job behind. The good news is that everyone knows your business . . . and the bad news is that everyone knows your business.

Working with intimates requires a unique set of skills and honest accountability. When joining a family business or any small company, the rules don't always emanate from HR. The short cuts that one has with a coworker who is also your relative can be a very good thing, or might make you feel stuck and pigeonholed in a role you'd hoped to outgrow. Often, your specific talents (and dreams) do not perfectly match the specifics of family business. But a good offer is a good offer, and make sure you can better that career opportunity before you turn it down. Every job will require adjustments. And you will always have to work hard and be flexible. Don't let the less formal construct of a family business soften or entitle you to become a lesser version of your working self.

Occupation: Artist

If you have ever dreamed of being a writer, or painter, or a performer and want to shine as an artist, take advantage of this in-between time and give that creative calling a shot. The artist's path may not be a practical way to sustain yourself financially, as your dad repeatedly told you when you graduated with Honors and a portfolio filled with glorious watercolors, being an artist won't buy the baby new shoes.

Once you've considered your financial needs, found some "ME" hours, asked your friends to be supportive, and begun to create, then you are an artist. Even if you can only create music or write part-time, do not be sheepish about calling yourself a working artist. Own your time and space, and make this passion come true.

How Did SHE Do It?
She and her mate made a deal with each other.
Karen C., artist married to fellow artist, two kids, Brooklyn pioneers

Karen met her husband right out of college in Brooklyn when they were both struggling artists. Both were quite talented, and they were a great match. In love and protective of each other's artistic dreams. But, once they had kids and diapers and tuition kicked in, they needed a new plan. Together they made a plan: they would trade off being artists. Only one could do so at a time; and the other partner had to have a job that gave the family health insurance.

Somehow, this very overt bargain actually worked. Mom and Dad alternated; one was always a freelance artist and the other a full-time employee with family benefits. Perhaps neither of them achieved their greatest potential either as an artist or as a careerist. But their marriage is fantastic, and their home and kids are terrific. Today, after years of playing studio music for others, her husband's own music is finding a real audience; and Karen still finds time to design furniture on the weekends but also has just been promoted to head of HR at a large advertising firm. They compromised and in life's big picture, they prevailed.

If you just want a little supportive push out of your creative funk, *STEAL LIKE AN ARTIST: Ten Things Nobody Told You About Being Creative* by Austin Keon will make you smile. Keep it by your bedside or in the bathroom for a fun pick-you-up.

"*YOU CAN DO IT!*"
—Lauren Catuzzi Grandcolas, *The Merit Badge Handbook for Grown-Up Girls*

Whether it's scuba diving or gardening or planning family events, this book is the most comprehensive guidebook for women to rebuild their passion into a profession. Pick any of the sixty specific paths, and YOU CAN DO IT! Catuzzi Grandcolas will introduce you to prominent mentors in that field.

Best Books and Links to Specific Job Hunts:

The very best book ever written about being your best artist self is *The Artist's Way* by Julia Cameron. Originally published in 1992, this is a twelve-week journaling self-help program that guides your artistic self into higher creativity. If you are stuck trying to find your creative mojo, *The Artist's Way* is your answer. The method and its tendrils of support groups are groundbreaking and very effective.

- http://www.learnhowtobecome.org/
- *You Can Do IT!*—Lauren Catuzzi Grandcolas

POLITICS

- *Getting a Job in Politics, And Keeping It*, Ben Wetmore (Creative Place Independent Publishing Platform, 2010)

WRITERS

- http://www.livewritethrive.com/2014/11/03/9-books-aspiring-writers-must-read/

LAWYERS

- *The Young Lawyer's Jungle Book: A Survival Guide,* Thane Josef Messinger

DOCTORS

- *Becoming a Doctor: From Student to Specialist, Doctor-Writers Share Their Experiences*, Lee Gutkind (W. W. Norton, 2011)

EDUCATORS

- *Teach Like a Champion: 49 Techniques That Put Students on the Path to College*, Doug Lemov (Jossey-Bass, 2010)
- http://drjimer.tumblr.com/post/34842249673/7-for-friday-good-reads-for-aspiring-educators

ENTERTAINMENT

- *Breaking Into The Biz: The Insider's Guide to Launching An Entertainment Industry Career*, Jenny Martin (Creative Place Independent Publishing Platform, 2013)

Daily Do List

❑ Took the Am-I-or-Am-I-Not-an-Entrepreneur test.

❑ Listed a Professional Hero; bought their book or read about them online.

❑ Officially embraced being freelance or artist or student.

❑ Spent ten extra minutes organizing or neatening a corner of my life.

❑ KEPT my spirits up and KEEP applying!

Hour Four
Follow-Up and Find The Outfit

Even though you only need to find ONE right job, you need to send out twenty-five feelers to get that one right job. In fact, you might come across a posting of an available job that is only of marginal interest to you. However, still send in your résumé, follow up, and if you can, grab that interview.

You never know exactly what Human Resources is really looking for. You never know who may have resigned from the company that very morning. Get out of the house. See how America works. You never know who you might run into in the elevator or getting coffee around the corner. Every interview has potential. Every interview is practice.

DISCOVER backdoors to heavily fortified castles. CHARM the gatekeepers.

J. D. Salinger's *The Catcher in the Rye*—which has sold over sixty-five million copies and is lauded as one of the three most important books in American literature—was originally rejected both by the *New Yorker* and by the publishing company Harcourt, Brace. The *New Yorker*'s editors criticized Holden Caulfield as being unbelievable, and the publisher thought Holden and his author were insane.

What I like about the story of *Catcher's* rejections is that it makes you realize: "The Gatekeepers aren't Gatekeepers. They have the Gate, but there is no fence around the gate . . . They are standing at some door, but the best things just walk around the door." The quote is by J.D. Salinger.

There is always a strategy to getting around the Gatekeeper.

When you are outside the Castle walls, the moat seems unbridgeable and the front door unbreachable. But there is always a porous portal to get to the inside. With charm and strategic persistence, you can become a welcomed invite. Every dream job requires a different approach. Be current with all that is going on, specifically with your Fave Five. If you want a job in finance, subscribe to the *Wall Street Journal* and check out part-time MBA programs. If you want to work for a housing contractor, walk the aisles of Home Depot for innovations. If you want to get into broadcasting, make a funny video and link it to the station's recruiter. It will take some creative problem solving, but it is important to remember that until you are fully rejected from a job, there is still a way in.

How To Charm The Gatekeeper:

- If you haven't been to your Fave Five brick-and-mortar space, pay a visit. Be friendly to the receptionist, but not creepy friendly. Don't go overboard, but a sugary bribe is often appreciated.
- If you sent your résumé and cover letter to the HR person, but not directly to the specific person you dream of working for, double up on sending. And vice versa. Take a second shot. You might need to update and personalize the cover letter with a new tidbit about yourself or the company.
- If you've sent and met and thanked them for the first interview, find a way to say hello and reintroduce yourself.
- Go to the company's, or store's, or school's websites and surf around. Usually there is a "Meet the Team" or an "About Us" section. See if you may know someone else who works there.
- Keep up with their social media postings on Instagram, Facebook, LinkedIn, Twitter. When you hear about something flattering or noteworthy, use it as a reason to pass along a nice note . . . it will push your résumé to the top.
- Multiply your reach for a potential job by inquiring about a program, event, or initiative the company is sponsoring. Shoot off a hello.
- If something new has happened to you that might align with them in an interesting way, find a way to sideways brag to them. Maybe they will see you in a new light.
- Keep networking. Ask your contacts and your Core Four if they know anybody who knows anybody.
- Reach out to your support network for any helpful pathways they might have to side-step the blockade.

Finally, be honest with yourself. It's good to be emboldened by rejection . . . to a point. At some junction, the quest for that specific job becomes a waste of your time. If you've hit that place, and you've gone that extra 10 percent . . . Next. Close the door yourself and move on.

> *"There is a crack in everything, that's how the light gets in . . ."*
> —Leonard Cohen

Reach-Out Exercise: GET YOURSELF AN INTERVIEW OUTFIT.

Make sure you buy ONE new piece to wear to the interview. There is a good chance you will not still fit into your old work clothes, nor will they still be style-appropriate. While it might be nice to get an entirely new wardrobe look, that really isn't necessary yet. Just one part of your outfit needs to be new—maybe a scarf, shoes, or a belt. One piece of newness should be enough to make you feel you are embarking on your next chapter.

Another fun pre-interview exercise is to dress up in your interview clothes and practice wearing them when you drop your son off at school, when you pick up the dry cleaning, and even when you walk the dog. Monitor how being dressed up makes you feel and enjoy the reactions you get wearing those pumps and fishnet stockings. Start projecting yourself in public in a new light.

Daily Do List

❑ Strategized an alternative way around the Gatekeeper.

❑ Practiced confidence by mastering my pitch.

❑ Gathered an interview outfit. Modeled it out in public.

❑ Kept sending out feelers and scheduling interviews.

Hour Five
Let's Enjoy the Interview!

Finally, and at long last, you landed an interview. Enjoy this first interview. Aim for your second.

Pre-interview Jitters: Rewrap Yourself as a Gift to the Employer.
Before you sheepishly walk into any interview, you need to mentally reframe the stage you are entering. Untangle your self-image: you are deserving, you are a catch. Psych yourself with the reminder that they have to hire someone, and they would be lucky if that someone was you. It is not a fluke that you have made it this far to the interview, and the company has a spot that they need to fill. The employer/interviewer/boss is looking for a win also. Job interviews are two-way streets. This is your moment to be that "win." Everybody is looking for someone to make their lives easier.

Visualize your best self being:

- Productive in this setting and filling in the company's blank spots.
- Spending many long hours enjoying this particular team.
- Foreseeing an interesting future within these walls.
- Advancing within the structure in front of you.

Try not to bring your nervousness into the interview. When you deliver your best self, you are a gift to a needy employer. They are ready to invest in a hire, so be that hire. Forget your ambivalence and pitch out your insecurities. You are prepared and practiced, and you can take control of this narrative. Enter joyously knowing that you are a valued commodity.

Reach Out: INTERVIEWING IS THE MOTHER OF ALL REACH-OUT EXERCISES.

- Dress up in your previously chosen office-appropriate outfit. Spit and polish your hygiene—try to wash out the gray, polish the nails, and lose a couple of quick pounds. Most important, look your best and wear what makes you most comfortable. Also, do some recon about the projected office spirit and dress code. Google as much as you can about the scenario you will be entering. Check with anybody you know who has worked there, or in an industry-similar office. You don't want to show up in a suit and heels to a running shoes manufacturing company . . . nor would you wear a sundress into a city law office.

- Get to the interview on time. Know where you are going exactly. Pad the drive with some extra traffic time cushion. And then add another ten minutes for parking issues. Your tardiness will be noticed, and you do not need the extra stress. In fact, if you are nervous, I would suggest getting to the interview early. Take a few calming breaths and exhale. Allow time to take a freshening stop in the ladies' room.

- This should be fun. If you are nervous or miserable, it will show. Try to look at this interview as a new audience. For a change, a grown-up will be listening to you and interested in what you have to say. This should be a test you are prepared for. You are equipped with a seasoned elevator pitch, and now that you have more than sixty seconds to deliver that pitch . . . relax.

- Expand your practiced pitch into an engaging conversation.

- Try to include a narrative story about yourself. Anecdotes are always what are most remembered.

- And engage your interviewer with questions about themselves. The more conversational and confident you appear, the greater the comfort zone in the room. Your positive spirit can become a force.

- Try to leave the room with a call to action. Either a promise to forward the hiring manager additional information or a pathway to another interview.

- Always, always follow up with a thank-you note or email.

The purpose of this first interview is to get asked back for a second interview. We want them to want you. We want them to call you back to the next level. Try to leave the interview room with a clear call to action for your next step. It's okay to even ask about a time line, expectations, and follow-up strategy.

If you get a sinking postinterview feeling that you may have botched this impression . . . Do not get too upset. "My bads" happen all the time . . . we have all flubbed an interview. It's okay to replay the interview and make a collection of all your bungled moments, your misspeaks, unasked questions, and missed opportunities. Don't kick yourself too much, just load all your errors into the "learning experience" pile and rename that meeting a practice run for your next interview.

Daily Do List

❑ Dressed my best and in keeping with the style of the office.

❑ Was not late.

❑ Turned my floating fear into adrenaline.

❑ Had fun being asked questions and asked questions myself.

❑ Wrote a memorable thank-you note.

❑ Amused my Core Four recounting the interview.

Step Seven
WHILE YOU ARE WAITING

"If you can keep your head when all about you/Are losing theirs . . ."
—Rudyard Kipling

The challenge of this step is to keep your spirits up. This segment of your journey can be the most taxing, and you may need to seek out cheers and support. You've been dutiful and diligent in the assignments of the past six weeks, and now the waiting and the doubling-back exercises are upon you.

You deserve real praise for putting in the hours, but know you're not quite there yet. And the waiting game isn't exactly a party. You have sent out dozens of résumés and inquiries, emailed all your connections, doubled back on all your resources, and still, no easy offer has surfaced. So now what? Do you wait for the phone to ring? It's all too easy to sink into fear and insecurity. Take a few breaths, break a sweat at the gym, double down on your outreach, and summon your grit.

Remember, you only need one "yes." While you're waiting for it, do your best to stay busy, maintain your daily-do habits, tend to your résumé with touch-ups, and try to remain positive in the face of what could be a whole lot of rejection.

Work stimulates your momentum. Work gets you out of your funk. Work fires you up into a more interesting candidate. Before a job comes through, do as much as you can to actuate a working attitude.

Also, it's a smart and positive move to bulk up your résumé with your most current professional details, even if they are part-time, volunteering, or interning. The more people you interact with in your chosen field, the more you expose yourself to like-minded folks, the more you can network and, ultimately, land that job.

Still often, your hard work and deserving profile do not immediately bear fruit. It will probably take longer than you would like to land the job. It's time to reconvene with your moxie and gather your gumption. You might want to enroll in a course that will enhance your skills, or sign up for a networking mixer that you have been hiding from. Volunteer for a job in your field of passion. Find a workshop and actually *go* to it. Clear away, or prevent stagnation by rousing yourself into the working world.

Hour Goals

Hour One:	Work for peanuts. Gain experience!
Hour Two:	Get educated.
Hour Three:	Maintain your mental health balance.
Hour Four:	Spy on the updated markets—Take a millennial to lunch.
Hour Five:	Savor your Mom life—The scenic journey won't last forever.

Start Your Job Before You Get the Job

The interview went well, you wrote a lovely thank-you note, and you were asked back for a second interview with your potential boss. Even though there were no red flags and the company hasn't yet filled the position, you still haven't received an offer, so now is the time for another push.

Reach-Out Exercise: WHAT ELSE CAN I DO TO GET NOTICED?

Call the hiring manager, ask an inside source, or replay the interview for a next step hint. Try to predict what assignment you might be given on day one of the job. Try to fulfill a hypothetical need that the company might have, and spec out that project:

- Design a new company logo.
- Pitch a new angle for an upcoming presentation the boss is preparing.
- Find a potential space for their expanding product line.
- Suggest a talent or new writer idea for a project they pitched.

Send in your pitch as if you were starting the job. Let them know you know what to do, and that you'll work hard to make their lives easier, even when you aren't asked. Prove that you can take initiative and push that ball down the field. Follow any published company news to show you can be a loyal, inside girl.

How Did SHE Do It?

She went that extra mile for free . . . and she was patient.

Alisa J., single mother, segment producer, Hoboken, NJ

Alisa was always the smartest in her class. She went to an Ivy League college and graduated magna cum laude in poetry. She found a career in copywriting and journalism, but writing for money was never fulfilling. Years went by, she met somebody interesting, had a baby, and moved into a grown-up apartment. When she began teaching her young daughter to read, she discovered she had a knack for tutoring. It turned out that tutoring was the perfect occupational filler for her few extra hours. She was good at it, it was lucrative, her students were *mostly* fun, and the parents were grateful.

As her child became more independent, Alisa began searching for full-time career opportunities. She wasn't yet desperate to rush into the forty-hour-a-week workforce. She wanted to be strategic and find a job that valued her talent, passions, and schedule.

Often, as she walked her Hoboken neighborhood, the show *Cake Boss* was being filmed. Her curiosity sparked, Alisa became an enthusiastic student of reality TV. Bingo! She wanted to become a part of what most enchanted her: real people accepting real challenges on national TV. Not an easy field to break into, but Alisa was determined. She knew people in the industry and asked for advice: one alumnus from her college was an executive at a production company; a mom from her daughter's preschool had been on an episode of *The Apprentice*; and Mr. Cake Boss himself was always happy to talk. It was an uphill climb of educating herself, networking, and trying to impress production companies to hire her. Alisa realized that her résumé, interviews, and smart friends were not enough; she needed to be able to give the company something that could help them make a reality show.

After two years of tracking down various leads, she sat down, wrote out a *Bible* plan for a particular show she had interviewed for the previous year. They didn't hire her for the first season, but just when they were prepping their second season, her plan landed on their desk, and an offer came through. She went the extra mile to become a *Mom for Hire* in her ideal job.

While being a single mom is not in Alyssa's original life plan, she has worked out a shared custody arrangement that suits her work pattern. With cooperative planning, Alyssa now has many hours, even days, when she has absolutely no parenting responsibilities. These swaths of free time have given her the space to focus on promoting her own career. While it would have been nice if her marriage had succeeded, being a single parent required both parents to formalize a positive partnership around their child's well-being. And eventually, everyone was better for it.

Keep Bracing Yourself: It Might Take Longer Than You Think...

Even for Sheryl Sandberg... In 2001, Sheryl Sandberg, COO of Facebook, had a dream instinct that "technology was transforming communication and globally changing lives." As Sheryl explains, "When the Clinton Administration ended, I was out of a job and decided to move to Silicon Valley. I gave myself four months to find a job but hoped it would take fewer. It took almost a year."

Why Women Feel They Are Being Rejected by the Marketplace

Employers are more likely to favor candidates with more traditional, linear résumés; it's easy to prejudge a woman who has taken a more "scenic path" to her career. In 2010, the Center for Work-Life Policy found negative attitudes about women taking time off from the workplace to be a major hiring block for recruiters and potential employers.

One female headhunter and mom from a large recruiting firm in Anaheim, California, explained that her corporate clients would "Rather poach a candidate then hire someone who has been out of work for even 9 months. Even if you have been working as a 'consultant,' your stock goes way down because you haven't had to answer to a boss or the system."

There's that prickly gatekeeper again.

Will Work for a... Job!

While I believe you should always, always, always be compensated for your work, I am not that naïve. As a mother and independent producer, there are many things I do every day for free.

I do not get paid to raise my children, nor do I always get paid to develop movies and TV shows—so much of what I do is on spec. In fact, I researched, interviewed women, and took years to write *Moms for Hire* with no compensation! Plenty of women needed a guidebook and I had a picture in my head of what *Moms for Hire* could look like, but I'd never written a book. I had never tried to get an agent or a publisher. I did believe I had a worthy project and a needy audience, so I kept at it, even with years of discouragement and rejection, and years of learning many new skills.

How Did SHE Do It?
She kept pushing through her own ceiling.

Hillary Rodham Clinton

In an interview on MSNBC's Hardball (January 6, 2016), Chris Matthews asked Hillary Clinton about her life/work path and her stumbles. Her revealing response gave a comforting boost to my own wonky self-esteem. Apparently, a huge hurdle in Hillary's career path was how she chose to describe herself; she had the "hardest time saying 'I Am ME.'" Yes. Even Hilary Rodham Clinton.

Through decades of what seemed like fabulously impressive education and careers (1st Student Graduation Speaker in Wellesley College history; Yale Law Review; Always the family breadwinner until White House, etc). Yet, even Hillary Clinton never felt she fully owned her own ambition. With all her absolutely legit accomplishments, in her mind, she was first "Bill's Wife" and then "Chelsea's Mom." Don't we all know that feeling.

With some brilliant prodding from Chris Matthews, Hillary nodded that it wasn't until her world was traumatized during "Bill's second administration's problems," according to Chris—that she was forced to redefine herself. The moniker of being Bill's wife had become too limiting (and painful) a description. Once Hillary could say "I am Me," then she could ask the people of NY to support that "ME" as senator. Finally, she allowed herself the gauntlet of "I can dare to compete . . . I can rise to this occasion." Once she had to advocate for herself, she could own her own deserving ambition. And now she is the leader of the Free World. Wow.

Inevitably, sometime in your life you will be hit by a terrible moment. Everybody—not only the reckless and unhealthy—will have to live through a primal tragedy of some variety. We are human. We are mortal. We make mistakes. It's inescapable. The key to a good life is how we cope with it, and then reframe ourselves out of those "second administration problems." Some say "you gotta hit rock bottom." Others say, "It's always darkest before the dawn." Often you have to be perched on a "cataclysmic edge" before you can see your own potential triumph. You will never be able to avoid all of life's bad things. Instead, allow tragic moments to liberate you and give you a boost to a new chapter.

Whatever provokes you out of your shell, find it. When rejection and painful moments hit you, do not wallow in victimhood, become your own advocate. You need to find YOU, before you can become your best self.

Most of all, it took years of relying on my inner positive encouragement and the positive pushing of my Core Bossy Girlfriends to keep me forging ahead. I discovered things about myself that didn't thrill me: I am not a natural organizer, nor am I a fast writer. I circle back around too much and can rewrite the spirit out of a snappy, smart idea. Also, I do not enjoy working alone; I get cabin fever in my own head.

By the time I realized that writing this book might not tap into my best skill set, I was too deep into it. I could not find a project partner, nor could I delegate finishing this book I had initiated, tirelessly sold, and resolutely believed in. I had to finish this without a big staff or even a partner to fill in my blank spots. So I sat down every day and spent many uncomfortable hours in the trench of my ergonomic chair. Every now and then I'd get a hum of accomplishment and creative pleasure, but being a rookie writer was a slog. Hopefully, it was worth it.

More often than I would like to admit, both as a film producer and writer, I've dipped into my own pocketbook to option a book; or hired a designer to help me with a pitch book for a prospective TV series; or, I would share my future profits with a partner who could help me with a project. I always invested in my creative happiness, and even if the reward is not always as obvious as a financial win, I insist that I always found value in the creative effort. DO NOT GIVE UP! Keep at it . . . there is a win in your future.

Pre-Job Your Job: Actualize Your Dreams

While those dozens of prospective employers are reviewing your résumé, do something every day that whets your back-to-work appetite. Work part-time; volunteer; seek out adjunct work: all these help build your professional credits. Volunteering or part-time work is not only critical in building your résumé, but it will also help you become a hands-on expert in your field of dreams. It might not be the sexiest part of your daily dos, but it gets you closer to where you want to be.

Get Moving

- Work for free.
- Work for a trial period.
- Offer to consult in your dream career.
- Intern for a little bit in the mailroom or equivalent.
- Go to the gym.
- Stay social; do not hibernate!

" When there are no ceilings, the sky's the limit. "
—Hillary Clinton

Daily Do List

❑ Reached out for part-time work or internship.

❑ "Spec-ed" out assignment for potential job.

❑ Followed up with contacts and connections.

Hour Two
Pad Your Résumé—Gain Experience!

Unemployment begets unemployment, which is why you have to act like you have a job before you actually have one. Add structure to your day by taking action that rolls you into your next chapter.

No one's knocking on the door, no one's ringing the bell . . . Your new job is not going to seek you out while you're Netflix-marathoning on your couch. *You* need to find the job and be your best advocate. Sometimes the route is circuitous. Don't be afraid to dive into new ways of networking, honing, crafting, and updating your skills.

Get Cracking, Girlfriend.

- ENROLL in Extension Classes.
  - Most cities have adult classes, many especially geared to retraining and reentry. Check out your local community college, state schools, and even "Ivies" have online courses. One friend is earning her Master's Degree from Harvard without leaving the comfort of her home in Los Angeles.
- FIND a workshop community specific to your passion.
  - Search for local writers' workshops.
  - Discover cooking clubs.
  - Join a trade union league.
- VOLUNTEER your talent
  - Internships are usually a catch-all phrase for corporate volunteering. But if the company has a good Internship Program, yes please.
  - Offer your sweat equity to anyone in your field of interest.
  - To volunteer for an NGO Charitable Foundation, go to www.volunteermatch.com, plug in your city and your cause, and this fabulous website connects your dots.
- JOIN a job-search support group—job support groups are everywhere. Start at:
  - www.fiveoclockclub.com
  - www.job-hunt.org
- www.40plus.org
- KEEP CURRENT. If you are a legal or medical professional, try to maintain your credential status. This often means continuing to pay fees and perhaps take some updating tests.

- As an alumni, Reach Out to your college career center. Their database is usually a goldmine.

Or you can Google your particular interests: fashion, manufacturing, horses, movies—there are Facebook groups and gatherings in every specialty. Friend strangers who like what you like. Join. Join. Join.

Meanwhile, keep returning to your Fave Five ideal job contacts and offer yourself up for an internship or a part-time position or even a trial internship. Don't give up.

How Did SHE Do It?
She always always volunteered and finally got compensated.
Deb B., widowed mom of teenage son, jewelry designer to development executive, Los Angeles

Deb has lived in Los Angeles for over thirty years. She is a fine jewelry designer who happily created her stunning pieces in her home studio while raising her toddler. When her husband died tragically in a fluke airplane accident, Deb was forced to reinvent her life as a single mom. Every emotional and financial step was a challenge, and—understandably—it took Deb many years to find her footing. She had to work to support herself and her son, but finding "satisfying" work was a luxury she could not yet afford. Deb kept up her jewelry business, but it was near impossible to make a sustainable living on one artist's income. After nursing her dad through an illness, she found part-time work as an independent health care manager, and her spirited personality and efficiency skills made her an excellent advocate for ill patients.

When Deb managed to get her son some financial aid at a Los Angeles private school, she immediately began volunteering to raise the school's scholarship funds. She soon discovered she was especially good at asking for money, a "transferable skill" she had mastered since her husband's death. Through great teamwork, the fundraising events increased the school's giving drive by $500K. Bravo to Deb and her team.

Deb was as surprised as anyone that she had such a talent for fundraising and for leading a team. She hadn't used either of those skills in her previous career as a jewelry designer. It turns out that while Deb was "not working," she had become an expert in

Continued . . .

many things: advocating for her son's education, always volunteering for every team and school outing, compassionately tending to folks struggling with various sicknesses, and forcing herself to socialize when all she wanted to do was stay home under the quilts.

One of the bonuses of becoming a stellar fundraiser was that it put Deb on the radar of the school board. Volunteering gave Deb a new lease on a new career path and exposed her to an elite network she might never have encountered. And in a testament to a full circle karma, she met people-who-knew-people, and Deb was recently offered a paid job at a local NGO that provides funding and support for at-risk LA children. A perfect fit for a deserving job candidate. Bravo again and again.

Surprisingly, Deb did a lot of work on herself: she dug through her grief, discovered several latent skills, and volunteered her resilient personality over and over until she found a new rewarding, paying career. And although it doesn't always pay for her teenage son's braces, she still gets to enjoy designing jewelry for a cadre of special clients. Win. Win. Win.

Get Out of the House

It is invaluable for you to start working outside the house. Even if it is part-time or volunteer work, you have broken the seal of being homebound. Your kids might moan and make fun of you for volunteering at their old nursery school, but you are loving it. They need to start adjusting to you not always being around. They may even become more self-sufficient and start cooking dinner for the family. A girl can dream.

<u>**Daily Do List**</u>

❏ Joined networking group and went to Job Fair.

❏ Amped up my résumé and creds with more academic experience.

❏ Networked with other support group acquaintances.

❏ Continued "spec-ing" out work for applications still in play.

❏ Checked in for an uplift and a reality check with my Core Four.

Hour Three

Chin Up!
Take Control of Your Own Mental Health

So, How Do I Not Go Bonkers?

It is lousy, but you should expect rejections. It is a guarantee. Sorry. You will be passed on plenty of times. Perhaps your résumé needs some more tweaking. Or your cover letter is too long. Or your recommendation was never sent. Or they hired someone else. Or it was simply the wrong job for you. Or you were the wrong person for the job.

Brace yourself to not win every job. It's always helpful if you can find out why they passed on you. Be brave and stick your neck out. If you are willing to listen, there is plenty to be learned from a professional recruiter and the honest HR person. It's worth a phone call to politely ask for some insights and advice. Also, it promotes a relationship with a frontline resource in the Career business. If you can get any of them rooting for you, doors will open.

Learn from every rejection.

Being a Squeaky Wheel is M'Okay.

Girls are too often raised to be game and go with the flow. It won't happen overnight, but the more you speak up and feel deserving of a break, a date, a job . . . the more appealing you become.

I was raised in a charismatic family of six boisterous siblings. We all always wanted some extra attention, and if you didn't fight for yourself at the dinner table, you'd miss your chance at dessert. If you didn't stake a claim in the Woody Wagon, you'd be stuck in the back-facing trunk. I quickly learned the absolute truth of: "The squeaky wheel gets the most grease." As I grew into the adult world, I prided myself on having a fair and generous nature; I know that honey helps everything, but sometimes, you've got to squeak, too. I am always strategizing how to get the most out of any situation. Often, when I check into a hotel, I first try to charm the tired-and-bored receptionist, and then if things are going well, I will ask: "Can I just have the third room?" A puzzled look might pass their face . . . so I smile and follow with, "I mean the room you are going to give me when I complain about the first two." You need to always project charm and a feeling of conspiratorial entitlement. If there is a better room for the same price, you deserve it. If you don't ask for the upgrade, no one is going to offer it.

To me, being labeled a "Bad-Ass" is a huge compliment. Get to know and celebrate your own swagger. Everyone is great at something . . . and everyone deserves a bigger piece of the glory.

How Did SHE Do It?
She hurdled a few steps by going back to school.

Michelle G., mother of second grader, former executive assistant

Michelle was a crackerjack assistant for an executive in the music business. She had a likable drive and an acknowledged eye for musical talent. Her sass and beauty were noticed by many, and an older established music executive saw Michelle and fell in love. They got married and had a son. When their son went off to kindergarten, Michelle tried to get back into the music world, but neither her résumé nor her connections could earn her anything past a low-paying assistant job. She felt ready for a leap.

Nothing could transcend her Mom Out Gap (her MOG). So Michelle borrowed some money and went to business school, and just as she was being offered a lucrative, corporate MBA-appropriate job, she was finally offered a job in Project Development at an independent record label, the very position she had been trying to get for years. Her current job does not use one ounce of her business school knowledge, but still, Michelle believes she would never have made it out of the secretary pool to full-time creative executive status had she not been certified with a master's degree.

Best Directional Advice EVER: Go 10% Further

I live in LA and drive a lot. Also, as a family we love our road trips. Five hours to San Francisco, easy. Fourteen hours to Colorado, better than two flights. Miles of country roads across New England, Americana road-tripping at its finest. We love driving places. But even with assists from assorted GPS apps and Waze . . . I still get lost way too often. And every time I find myself doubting my whereabouts, I remember a favorite mom mantra: "When you feel most lost, don't stop or retreat . . . Always, always go ten percent further." Uncertain and confused, you are convinced you've passed your destination. However, in most cases, you just haven't yet arrived . . . and going ten percent beyond your spot of lost panic will do the trick. Etch this advice into your *Mom for Hire* dashboard: always go ten percent further. Try to be ten percent better. Work ten percent harder. More often than not, you are not yet lost. You just need to keep going.

DEB TELLS ALL

Failure actually is an option.

When my editor asked who I was hoping would write the foreword for this book, I gave her two names of great women I knew quite well and were excellent moms and writers. When they asked if I knew anybody else, I boldly suggested the country's First Mom, who off-ramped her own career eight years ago: Michelle Obama. At the start of the administration, Mrs. Obama announced that she would not take any official role and would tend to her kids and her home. Sure, behind the scenes, she accomplished a lot from her FLOTUS perch but never took on an official capacity. I knew I was aiming for the highest of high stars. But I believe that the five and a half million stay-at-home moms would find tremendous comfort in the First Lady's reflections.

I wrote asking an interview and asked a few tentative connections to forward my request to their people in the White House. I reached back to past connections, book agents, big donors . . . everyone. Quickly, I heard many absolute NOs:

- "She can't do anything while still in office" . . . *but the book won't published until the Obamas leave the White House.*
- "If she said 'yes' to you, she couldn't say 'no' to someone else . . ." *But she has already written for Lena Dunham's blog* Lenny, *acted on NCIS, etc.*
- "It's not how the First Lady wants to message herself" *Okay, but eight years ago, she did announce that she was opting-out. . . . so any updated thoughts would be welcomed.*
- "She's very busy and wants to spend her free time with her girls." *Bingo . . . exactly why this beloved and brilliant woman could speak for us all.*

My contacts all advised me to give up the quest. They said, "It's never going to happen," and "you're being too pushy," and "stop wasting your time." Still, I had one long shot to take before I could give up gracefully. Direct mail. I wrote a very polite letter and sent it to her home at 1600 Pennsylvania Avenue. I am told it will take three months for an unsolicited letter to be processed, and by that time my publishing window will have closed. Yet I still have not officially been rejected. My slim hope is that I get lucky and whoever reads my interview request is also a Mom . . . and perhaps an interested advocate. Perhaps the letter will eventually find its way upstairs. Perhaps not, but you never know when a well-intentioned deed will boomerang back with a unexpected reward. To be continued. . . .

My takeaway remains the same: **Always aim high**; the worst that could happen is you get a rejection. **Always ask**; you are entitled to be ambitious. **Always keep trying**; even when discouraged, go 10% further.. And finally, **always have a Plan B;** be happy with your safety school.

Reach-Out Exercise: CLEANSE YOUR PALATE OF SELF-DOUBT AND REJECTION.

Whatever it takes to cheer yourself up: plan a holiday, cook a great meal, call a friend. Nobody wants to hire a moper. Unfunk yourself. Go back to your Application Tracker. Follow up on at least two outstanding applications. If they pass on you, be brave and ask for a helpful reason. It's the least a rejecting employer can do.

Use their feedback to make résumé tweaks; to go back and get some more experience; or recalibrate your interview presence. You are who you are, so don't expect to overhaul your persona and double your cred. Just tweak your components and confidently be the best version of yourself. And then remind yourself over and over: you are doing your best.

Daily Do List

❑ Return to my Application Log.

❑ Follow up with two "Asks."

❑ Add 3 new contacts from Facebook, LinkedIn, walking the dog, anywhere.

❑ Send five more feelers.

❑ Don't stop believin' in myself.

Hour Four
Spy on the Updated Markets—Take a Millennial to Lunch

> *"Be nosy . . . eavesdrop. Youths make the best spies. Find some."*
> —Jon Waters, To Parents, RISD Graduation, 2015

The older you get, the more chaotic the world seems. Don't fight the chaos . . . manage it. And if you need a millennial to explain the chaos, then reach out to one. They'll be happy to share. The workplace has modernized, and you need get "current-ized" on the latest everything: software, skills, industry habits, even new cultural norms.

While you were raising a family, the technology and business world bolted forward. So today, reach outside of your comfort zone, and begin catching up. For a speed lesson on all things *now*, take a millennial to lunch, or for a happy hour drink. Hopefully, you can find someone of another generation who has two or three years of work experience under their belt, but who has not yet begun a family. Question them about how they got their current job, their career path, and have them walk you through their day-to-day. This will give you some much-needed insight into the modern workplace. For example, offices with doors are a rarity . . . even some CEOs sit in a cubicle and take meetings in gathering rooms. Chairs are out; standing desks are the rage. Long lunches are out, and so is excessive overtime. Real work is now done in coffee shops and libraries. Out of town gigs, part-time, freelance, off-hour jobs are now the norm.

If you don't know a millennial, look one up at the company where you'd like to work, or a similar company. Cold-call a millennial and ask if they would give an hour of their time to give you the skinny on their days, their favorite podcasts, TV shows. People LOVE to talk about what they know. Oh, and pay for lunch. That always helps.

Reach-In/Reach-Out . . . A LAST HURRAH!

Whatever this means to you, take a day off. Go on . . . You deserve it!
Occasionally, it's okay to play hooky from the job hunt. While it is good to consider the *job of finding a job* to be *a job*, it cannot be all-consuming 24/7. And after hours, you need to close down the search. You deserve to take a break. See a movie. Take a nap, complete with drool. Go to the beach; get a massage. Take a long hike or bike ride. Tend to your garden. Applaud your efforts, even if they haven't yet brought you a dream offer. Do whatever it takes to unwind, restore, and decompress.

While the purpose of this is to give yourself a little minute to get your mind off all things *job*, it's also great for reflection and contemplation. Sometimes, while doing the mundane, you'll think up important things you otherwise wouldn't have—maybe about your career direction, maybe about some of the reach-in exercises you've done.

Refer back to your list of things you do during your "ME" time that you love, and claim a day of fun and rest for yourself.

Daily Do List

❑ Took a millennial to lunch. (They make great spies on the Now.)

❑ Refreshed my circuits with updated intel. Downloaded new podcasts. Bought *Wired*; subscribed to *Slate*.

❑ Signed up for Instagram . . . Maybe even Snapchat.

❑ Asked my Core Four for an ego boost.

❑ Kept up my to-do list and tidy-up minutes.

Hour Five
Savor Your Mom Life—A Job Has Arrived

You're Hired!

OMG . . . you got the job. A real offer! After months of maneuvering and working hard at the job-of-getting-a-job, at last, an offer comes in. Woo Hoo! Congratulations!

There is still plenty of in-between space between the *Day of the Offer* and your *First Day of Work*. Plenty of transitioning and negotiations will be needed on the home front and into your new office life.

Sometimes, there is a "switcheroo," and the offer you got hired for was not exactly the job you interviewed for. So it's a job, but not exactly the ideal job, and you may need to recalibrate yourself and your expectations.

Think of it as walking into Banana Republic on the hunt for a dress you really need. After scanning the entire store, there are no dresses in your size, but there are two great skirts on sale. And you remember you have a matching top at home. Be happy with your two skirts and make it work. You're not *settling*, just *adapting*.

Maybe you're finding yourself suddenly ambivalent with a sort of buyer's remorse. Oh, no. You have flashes of the job's imperfections and what you will be giving up by going back to work. Double "oh, no." What were you *thinking*?!? How can you really do this?

Maybe with your foot halfway in the door, you learn something somewhat troubling about your future company. Is it the way you were treated when you asked about vacation time, or a dress code policy? Are these legitimate red flags, or was the hiring manager having a bad day?

Often, a job for mom is an adjustment for the whole family. Suddenly, domestic tasks need to be more evenly distributed. And your shift in attention will absolutely create a back-draft; feelings of neglect and abandonment could be dramatic during the adjustment phase.

In truth, with all major life moves (marriage, home purchases, school choices), ambivalence can rear its ugly head. All potential triumphs require some measure of a leap of faith: Will they like you? Will you like them?

At this point, you've done a thorough job of weighing and reweighing the pros and cons. To make any progress, you have to gamble a bit. Often, you won't know if you made the right move until you jump in and test the waters for at least a few months.

Go for it. It's going to be better than okay, and maybe even terrific.

The following, final celebratory step will reinforce your powers of negotiation so that you get what you deserve.

However scary this next step is, you landed the job!!!! YOU DID IT! Let your ego have a par-tay. Go out for dinner with the family. Do a jig with your spouse. Loosen up your smile muscles.

Reach-In Exercise: IT'S OKAY TO FREAK OUT.

Take a minute to do some free association writing about your feelings, or call a friend and talk through this huge accomplishment, with all its risks and rewards. You need to be in top form for the last step, where you will sew together all the months of Steps and Exercises to become your own best champion.

CONGRATULATIONS!

Reach-Out Exercise: BRAG! CELEBRATE!

Write a note to yourself to commemorate your hard-earned offer. Look back at your picture frame and ideal job description. Call friends. Throw a party. Drop your doubts.

Daily Do List

❑ Absorbed the offer.

❑ Freaked out.

❑ Celebrated with family and friends.

Step Eight

YOU'RE HIRED! NOW WHAT!?

Hour Goals

Hour One:	Negotiate with artful entitlement.
Hour Two:	Acknowledge the void you left at home.
Hour Three:	Write a letter to yourself . . . and enjoy the honeymoon.
Hour Four:	Review First Day Tips.
Hour Five:	Give back and don't minimize your own job-hunt struggles.

Hour One
Negotiation 101

"*Let us never negotiate out of fear. But let us never fear to negotiate.*"
—John F. Kennedy

Always NEGOTIATE. The first task of your new job is to get the best deal you can. You deserve to be paid fairly, and it is important to you and your employer to make sure you feel valued. Although the employer's stance may be that thay they hold all the cards and that you are replaceable before you start, negotiating is a two-way street. Both parties are happiest when both feel the win.

Studies have shown that women and men are equally good at negotiating, but women are better at negotiating for others rather than themselves. Perhaps you were that girl who argued her way around the injustice of being graded on the curve for your 8th Grade midterms, or you never let your brother grab that extra piece of pie. But if you weren't always great at asserting yourself, today's the day to start. Summon your confidence, and decide to be worthy and entitled. Fake it if you need to, but just act like your deserve it.

Please, please, do everything in your soul to not take the negotiating stage personally. Negotiation is a sport like any other. You're championing for yourself. And the other side is just doing their job. That's all. Nothing more.

There are a few easy tips to help you get the amount you deserve.

- **Know Before You Go:** What is your worth? What is your midrange Blue Book value? Just like with housing prices, or car shopping, you can find comps that are ballpark matches of your services rendered. Plug into a few legit job sources (*Salary.com or TheSalaryExpert.com*) that calculate the value of your personal skills with the position you have been hired to do.
- Nowadays, there is an assigned hierarchy of job levels from intern to entry-level, to assistant, to manager, to director, to VP. Get a corporate salary range of what your specific job pays in the marketplace. Every company has its specific pay scale based on its specific job ladder, but you need to know what the parameters are, and then you should feel experienced about negotiating within that range.

- **Do Not Accept the First Offer:** After the company has made you their first offer, now you can go ahead and ask for what you want. Take note: if there is absolutely no give in their negotiation stance now, that is often an omen of their style of generosity to come. Every hiring partner wants to pay a pittance when hiring. However, what the hiring partner wants should be irrelevant to you. Likewise, it is also irrelevant that you need to be paid more money for your mortgage or your kid's braces. You need to hear their offer, and then say you want to think about it and prepare a counter. Remember, it's sport, not personal.

- **Be Ready to Give a Number That Makes Sense and Reflects Your Value.** If you have a strong interest in the job and the employer is a good fit, but the offer is not what you had hoped for, you can consider making a counteroffer proposal. If you decide to counter, don't counter on every single point. Think through, discuss with friends, and decide what are the one or two most important factors in the deal. Concede to something and hold firm on something else. If the salary is too low, yet you know the firm will not negotiate on salary, then counter with other important—not monetary—factors: health insurance (include dental and vision), vacation time, start date, bonus reevaluation (three, six, or twelve months), title, expenses, phone allowance, travel allowance, flex-time, telecommuting a certain number of days per week or month.

- **Be Reasonable.** Always be the one standing in the "fairness" camp. You need not ask for the moon, just an acceptable total pay package for your skills. And your counteroffer can include more than just a sign-on base pay. It can include bonuses, an early performance review, a signing bonus, relocation expenses, car allowances, computer, stock options, etc. Often these perks may not make that much of a financial difference, but it is very important to know that you can have a voice and be heard before you even sign that W-2 form. Start off your job from a position of strength.

- **Don't Be Greedy, Lady.** Just remember that you cannot attempt to negotiate the entire offer; you need to choose your one or two battles carefully, conduct your research, and prepare a short counterproposal. Avoid whining. Try to be sportsmanlike and gracious.

You might have to start at a lower salary (and job title) than you want, and maybe much less than your previous job. Ouch. Ouch. Only you know if it's worth the compromise. While it's been a while since you played hardball, you still have the moves. Avoid all doormats. Be prepared when you speak with your new employer, with a complete, prioritized summary of your ideal offer, and know in your mind how negotiable you're willing to be. If you feel undervalued, alert your Core Four and ask for a "You're worth a lot!" boost or consult experts in the industry to let them know you received an offer and need advice on how to handle the salary negotiations.

How Did SHE Do It?
She checked her ego and took a seat on the rocket ship
Phoebe K., mother of two teenage daughters, TV executive

For 20+ years, Phoebe was a valued executive at major cable network, and as the company prospered, so, too, did Phoebe's career. She rose from the casting department to live shows to scripted programming. Yet after two decades at the same organization, it was time to move on. Her exit was bittersweet, but Phoebe was given a severance parachute and time to regroup and find her next best thing.

Phoebe was determined to enjoy some new scenery during her time off; and she found a new love for parenting her teenage daughters. Finally, she could put away her phone and be present in her homelife. She had budgeted herself an off-ramp sabbatical and actively did not look for work for at least six months. And then, she methodically began scouting the new markets that might appreciate her talents and wisdom. She was thoughtful about her passions, her expertise, and what she offered as a job candidate. Phoebe had a keen understanding of teen spirits and their trends. Also, she shined in the corporate arena and wanted to make sure she was also given a seat at the big kids' table. Quite rapidly, she identified and listed her employable skills, her job requirements, and her professional pleasure zone.

She plugged herself into LinkedIn and after twenty years rewrote her résumé. She discovered that her adolescent audience had rapidly morphed and become cordless, and even though she'd only been away for months, she had a lot of catching up to do. She took many meetings and clicked with an old colleague who had just founded a digital media company. After a full year off the market, Phoebe got an offer she could not refuse as an executive at a digital start-up company. The offer came with less money, a lower title and she was the eldest member of the team. Bravo . . ?

Continued . . .

210

Phoebe made a conscious decision to put her ego away and to quickly soak up as much as she could about the mechanics of the modern digital world. She had to become an expert again, and every day she pinched herself not to complain. Her all-millennial team quickly came to rely on Phoebe's sagely advice. She was given more responsibilities and is again in command. Phoebe is genuinely happy with this new chapter in this updated industry, even though her salary has not yet risen to its previous level. Yes, she still deserves to be paid more. But for now, Phoebe is patiently carrying on as the loyal and innovative worker she's always been. Age has given her strength and wisdom. She knows what she deserves to be paid and is not shy about making her financial requests clear. Phoebe realizes even a very good job may never be the perfect job.

If you cannot get exactly what you feel you deserve today, there are other victories you can get when finalizing your deal. Many jobs come with a trial period (60, 90 days) in which your salary is tiered until you become a fully vested employee. Make sure the trial period is a two-way street so that if you decide the job cannot work for you, you are not committed, either. This makes the honeymoon period mutually exciting.

Finding the perfect job is always a miracle, but if you like what you do everyday, it gives you a sense of belonging and accomplishment, then be happy. Please.

"If you're offered a seat on a rocket ship, you don't ask what seat. You just get on."
—Eric Schmidt, former CEO of Google

Reach-In Exercise: WHAT'S YOUR BOTTOM LINE?

You'll be nervous when you counter, so fill out these line items, star your priorities, and keep it handy as a trusty cheat sheet.

What salary and perks are nonnegotiable?
_____

Net (take-home) salary. Cash money. _____

Flex-Time _____

Vacation Time _____

Insurance _____

Stock Options _____

Pension/401K _____

Computer _____

Expense Account _____

Relocation Expenses _____

Start Date _____

Bonuses _____

Reevaluation (three, six, or twelve months) _____

Title _____

Phone Allowance _____

Telecommuting _____

Car Allowance _____

Daily Do List

❑ Researched the specific comps for the job I was offered.

❑ Listed my "must haves" and my "can be okay withs."

❑ Proved I could advocate for myself.

❑ Waited for their proposal, and then devised a counter.

Hour Two
Acknowledge the Void You Left at Home

"If you want children to keep their feet on the ground,
put some responsibility on their shoulders."
—Abigail Van Buren a.k.a. "Dear Abby"

You officially have a job . . . with official hours and an official paycheck. Now, you can officially assign home duties to perfectly capable mates and children.

Fair Warning: This transition may not be pleasant for the home team. There will be an adjustment period for everyone, including you and the dog. Maybe the goldfish won't feel much of a shake-up, but expect some guilt-throwing, some acting out, and a few forgotten assignments. It could be a bumpy transition at home for a while.

Be prepared for random crankiness and other symptoms of "I don't like change" from your spouse and kids. It's pretty natural. Be prepared to get teased or even belittled by your sassy teens. Just roll your eyes and throw it back at them, "oh, you just don't get it." And, resist the flow of guilt. Never let anyone ever infer you are being a bad mom by re-upping your career.

When Lisa went back to work after nine months of severance leave, sixth-grader Stella's stomachaches began. Often twice a week, the middle school nurse called Lisa at work to let her know that Stella wasn't feeling well. We all know that a mom can only be as happy as her least happy child. Stella's sufferings were real and painful for her mom, and they definitely sidetracked any honeymoon period for Lisa at her great new job. Still, both mother and daughter kept listening and hearing each other. After a few up-and-down months, a successful volleyball season, and one perfectly extravagant family vacation, the stomach aches have stopped.

You'll need to compartmentalize your work life and home time. Clearly preplanning your five to ten hours away every day will require organizing that you didn't need to deal with pre-work. Childcare management will definitely change, and you may need to find an after-school daycare possibility, or hire an extra hand for folding shirts and driving the kids to activities. Remember, weeks ago you began dropping the chore bucket on your kids and spouse. Hopefully, the household has stopped grumbling and started actively contributing to the family's well-being, but if not, today is reckoning day.

Refer back to the Step 4 giveaway exercise chart. You might need to revise the Stars & Bugs Chart. Just as you are expecting a rewarding paycheck, your home boys and girls will be expecting (and hopefully earning) a bit more allowance.

It is absolutely normal to feel guilty about your new "away-ness." Likewise, it's pretty common if your child is feeling abandoned and genuinely anxious about your departure. Some of this is a real adjustment and requires extra sensitivity on your part, and some of it is—just—your own guilt that the kids pick up and capitalize on. Stay firm and confident in your choice, and the kids will follow in this mind-set. You're the captain of this ship, Mom.

A stay-at-home mom's always-around availability is a comfortable crutch for everyone. Now that you won't always be cushioning the nest, everybody will have to grow up a little and adjust. So, adjust. If you are still feeling conflicted, please read the recent Harvard study that says working moms raise more successful daughters and nicer sons. I know, I know . . . This thesis feels a little weaker when you are living with a bored nine-year-old and a cranky teenager who doesn't like the idea of doubling up on chores, but an Ivy League affirmation can help calm a conflicted soul.

Reach-Out: GIVE IT AWAY, GIVE IT AWAY, GIVE IT AWAY NOW.

Scan back through these exercises:

- *What Do I Do All Day?* Baseline Chart (Step One/Hour One).
- Mom Résumé (Step Four/ Hour One).
- Monthly Nut Calculation Chart (Step Four/Hour Three).
- Kids' Benchmark Tasks (Step Four/Hour Two).

Fill in the blanks for what you can train others in the house to take on. Every neatened corner, every organizational assignment, and every recreational charge can be parsed out.

Why do you always clean out the goldfish tank from the county fair win of four years ago, the one your little one had to have? Why are you waiting on hold for the cable company while your teenager is Snapchatting? Why is it your fault when the white pants get dyed purple when washed with the new sweatshirt? Or when the favorite duffel bag goes missing? You are not doing anybody any good by shielding them from cleaning up their own spilled milk or from putting away their own Halloween decorations, folding their clothes, doing the dishes, or taking out trash.

---

http://qz.com/434056/working-moms-have-more-successful-daughters-and-more-caring-sons-harvard-business-school-study-says.

Make it fun! This doesn't have to be an exercise in dread. Give assignments and remember that these things help launch your kids and make them more accountable later on. It's a huge disservice to do everything for your kids. They need to know that pitching in matters, whether you're working or not.

Today, list every task you perform to keep the family in a sustainable, happy place. Many (hopefully most) of these give you pleasure. Others take up too much of your bandwidth and now must be delegated.

MOM'S PLATE IS FULL!

My Plate   The New Chief

Every Day, Mom:

- _____   _____
- _____   _____
- _____   _____
- _____   _____
- _____   _____
- _____

Every Week, Mom also:

- _____   _____
- _____   _____
- _____   _____
- _____   _____
- _____

Every Month, it's Mom's thing to:

- _____   _____
- _____   _____
- _____   _____

Seasonally, every year, Mom:

- _____   _____
- _____   _____
- _____   _____

These tasks will not be set in stone and could vary as people grow. Download and print from my website!

How Did SHE Do It?
Surprised by tragedy, she took charge and reconfigured.

Marianne, single mother of two sons, public school teacher.

Marianne and Gordon were college sweethearts, and they had a plan. He was going to work on hyperdrive for twenty years nonstop, save up, and then retire when the boys were teens. She always wanted to work and was a beloved teacher in the New Jersey Public School system. She did her best to plan her pregnancies to coincide with the school year and was always ready to return to work after maternity leaves. She learned how to rejuvenate during her summer and school holidays and was proud of the life balance she had found. They were in sync in their values and child-rearing philosophy. They built a dream home in the suburbs, with a cherished wine collection and a well-tended backyard. They mowed their own lawns and washed their own bay windows. Sadly, one evening driving home from a late dinner meeting, the car lost control, and Gordo didn't make it out of the car.

Suddenly, Marianne's world had been turned upside down. She fiercely wanted to remain in the home she had built with her husband and where they had raised their kids.   But honestly, she had no idea of all the things Gordo had routinely taken care of. So she sat down and made a list of the specific tasks that her husband handled—from changing the air vent filters to coaching the soccer team to filing their taxes. A complete inventory . . . She installed Quicken into her computer and began paying the monthly bills; she realized their twelve-year-old son could figure out the sweeper and chemistry of the pool, and he always was a better foul shot coach than their dad. Check. And with a little negotiating, the ten-year-old would rake the lawn once a week and soon could handle the lawn mower . . . or they could hire a professional. Turns out, the younger son was a brilliant BBQ-er and loved to bake. So they would never starve.

List it. Delegate it. Onward. Everyone had to take it up a notch, and they were going to reboot as a revised family. A tragedy forced Marianne to draw up a list of what was on her plate, but devising and posting a Mom inventory is a great plan for all of us in calmer times, too. Until it is formulated into a list, it's all soft labor. Once you have a list of what needs to be done, you can prioritize and make the important things happen.

Daily Do List

❑ Listed all my "Mom tasks."

❑ Assigned a fair portion to all the capable members of the home.

❑ Posted the "assignment list" in a public spot.

❑ Devised a reward system for all assignments completed.

Hour Three
Kiss A Little Tush. Just a Little.

Write Yourself a First-Day-of-Work Letter.

I have never been a consistent self-improver. I am not an addictive person, so neither have my indulgences nor my exertions ever been obsessive. I like to have a good time, but I always remember the hangover. I've never hit rock bottom and haven't had to overhaul my whole life force. I've been pretty constant. I diet when I must and I exercise enough, but all in moderation.

I don't meditate every day, nor do I journal with consistency. I'm not one of those people who preschedules my hair coloring, and I wait for the dentist to tell me when I'm due for a cleaning. I buy organic when it's in front of me but don't insist on it regularly.

And yet, I am a big fan of punctuating certain occasions by writing a letter to myself. Every New Year's, I write a letter of intent. Seal it. Tuck it away, and open the time capsule the next New Year's Eve. These letters are part resolution/part wish-announcement/part state-of-the-year declaration.

Reach-In Exercise: CEMENT YOUR INTENT.

Today, the day before you embark on a new job, pause for a moment and grab a piece of paper to record this moment. Today is a very good day to punctuate your next chapter.

- How do you think this next career chapter will be rewarding?
- How do you predict your kids will handle this?
- How do you plan on spending your new income?
- How do you intend to work differently this time around?
- What's your fantasy expectation for this job?
- What will a *win* look like one year from this day?

Reach-Out Exercise: LICENSE TO INDULGE.

Buy yourself a congratulations present, and give your kids and family a perk, too. *Try to make the whole family feel as if they got a new job.* It will be so much easier if they feel like it's an all-family victory.

Daily Do List

❑ Wrote myself a letter about tomorrow's adventure.

❑ Bought myself a "Start Day" gift.

❑ Gave my family a bon voyage meal or surprise promise.

Hour Four

Write a Letter to Yourself. Advice to Your Daughter (and Son)

"Dress well. Go in early. Leave late. Always ask yourself what more can I do?"
—Jamie Cole, Summer Camp Owner & recent PR Executive

Reach-Out Exercise: YOUR LONG-VIEW STRATEGY.

Show up like you never left. . . . How to rock your "First Impression" on Day 1.

The smartest work advice I ever received was to just make sure your boss knows you are doing a good job. So simple, but not always so easy to achieve. Hopefully, by now you have done enough mutual vetting and you know the landscape of the job you are landing on. And usually your boss or coworker will give you your first assignment on day one. But even that is not always crystal clear.

Figuring out your second assignment and how you can do something that will make everybody's work life better is the best impression you can make. Muster all your ingenuity and flexibility and efficiency, and bring it. So, once you have completed your first task, be proactive and suggest a second assignment.

As a boss, I'm always looking for a worker who can make my life easier and make me look good. My biggest pet peeves are when someone whose salary I am paying asks or does the following:

- "What do you want me to do now?" *Figure it out.*
- They forget to complete a task, and I have to ask again. *Write it down. Your memory is supposed to be better than your boss's.*
- Asks "how do I solve this problem?" *Never present a "problem" unless you are simultaneously presenting a "solution."*
- Tell me they tried but got a no. *Never be the one to say no to your boss. Always give options. Say: "Sure you can have those extra ten bags of soil, but then you have to get two fewer orange trees."*

How to Make Your Boss Happy—and How to Make Friends

- Bring donuts (or bagels). Everybody loves donuts, and most people appreciate bagels.
- Okay to overdress during week one, but know the style and try to blend in.
- Fly under the radar: Don't let yourself get pigeonholed into a first-week quirk.
- Smile and watch the flow—don't be overly friendly or too noisy.
- Be a listener, not a gossiper.
- Don't brag too much about your kids. You were the one they hired, not the family package.
- Don't tell everyone your struggles with landing a job.
- If the company puts you through a training program, take it seriously. Glibness is a turnoff.
- Don't try to prove yourself too soon. Ask smart questions, but don't show off education, share brags, etc. Be likable first. Let someone else finish your crossword puzzle.
- Set up meetings with key people within the company, and show an interest in getting to know them. Learn everybody's name, even if you need to write them down. It's more awkward to have to ask twice.
- If you can, co-op a friend to show you the ropes.
- The goal is not to make enemies and hopefully get invited to something by Friday.

Most of the time you will get a grace period to celebrate. Even if it is hectic and the workload is too heavy, let the adrenaline give you some pleasure. People will usually be nice enough during this honeymoon period. Don't waste these precious positives. Don't second-guess good tidings. Try to coast a bit on the novelty of being back in the workforce.

Daily Do List

❑ Brought a treat and a smile to work on Day One.

❑ Listened and learned names and social codes.

❑ Enjoyed the honeymoon.

Hour Five

Pay It Forward

Although it might be boring to relive, do not forget the work you went through to get this job. Don't brush over the challenges of getting a job. It was a rough couple of months, or more, and you worked hard to arrive here. You persevered, and now you are gainfully employed. Now that those struggles are behind you, let's not minimize their toughness.

Throughout the years of formulating *Moms for Hire,* I interviewed women on every edge of the work-home pendulum. One of my target audience moms was a friend I had known for years as a proud and supertogether stay-at-home mom. Barbara had given up her legal practice and fully invested in shepherding her kids through high school and into elite colleges. And during those rearing years, Barbara's career had been on hold. Sure, she had remained current in politics and advocacy, but she feared she may have off-ramped for too long. When she finally dropped her youngest off at a top-notch university, Barbara began looking for a job in earnest. She did everything right: she upgraded her résumé, renewed her lapsed legal credentials, bought some great new dresses, networked her old and new contacts, leaned on a few of the men and women she had done part-time volunteer work with; and within seven months, Barbara was gainfully employed. I had clocked in many hours of listening to career confusions, and yet, when I interviewed the happy Barbara less than a year after she began her new job, she had no memory of those angst-filled years.

After just a season at her new job, Barbara had forgotten all feelings of her unemployed bewilderment and shame. I was stunned. She still is a lovely friend, but she had completely rewritten her narrative, and I had wasted hours listening to the horror of her lost professional status, her unappreciated life choices, blah blah blah.

My heartfelt request to all of you who trudged through these steps and finally succeeded is PLEASE be good enough to remember your struggle. PLEASE remember that jobs come and go, and the older we get, our happiness will rest on our power to help others as we were helped. Remain compassionate. There are plenty of other moms who need your encouragement and even your nightmare stories of woe and frustration. Without your cheering from the finish line, they might give up. Now that you have made it, be a humble heroine.

Once you've landed a job, it's easy to forget—like we all may have with the pain of childbirth—how long it took and how bad it sometimes felt. Try not to brush it all aside. When another mom comes along asking you for job advice, take the meeting. Become the mentor to their *Moms for Hire* journey. These women are your grassroots. Remember your struggles and that there are still plenty of folks who have not yet figured out a way back to meaningful work. If you'd like, buy them a copy of this book. Or just highlight your best secrets and become a bossy girlfriend to others. All advice is ultimately autobiographic, so now that you have succeeded, generously pass on your pathways to those still sitting in the carpool pick-up lane.

DEB'S FINAL TELL ALL

The Lost Boys Rise Again

Over a decade ago, the screenwriter Margaret Nagle had written a brilliant script about the Lost Boys of Sudan called *The Good Lie.* The movie had stalled out, but the script was still the same fantastic. Margaret, with my husband Bobby as the producer, had told the story of three Lost Boys and one Lost Girl who came from the same destroyed village in what is now South Sudan. These orphaned shepherd kids banded together, walked thousands of miles across Africa, and finally rested in Kenya's Kakuma refugee camp. Years later, the USAID allowed them to immigrate to Kansas City to try out their American Dream. At the Kansas City airport, the Boys were met by an adorable and well-meaning employment agency worker who has no idea of their circumstances or the difference between Sudan and Samoa.

Margaret had lived through a lot of no's in her life . . . but she always believed that "To move ahead, you only need one yes." After the script had been inactive for years, Margaret got it back from the studio that had originally developed it with Bobby, she found another interested financer, and got it to Reese Whiterspoon to play the Kansas City employment agent. Ta Da.

Years after Bobby's passing, a new life was born into this dormant project. And chalk It up to human decency or good karma: I was asked back into the fold as an executive producer. Since I had remained involved with many Lost Boys and Girls, my outreach contacts were valued, and my years of involvement with hundreds of Lost Boys gave me credibility with both the filmmakers and the Sudanese community. A plus to *The Good Lie* film project was that we established a fund to reinvest in the Lost Boys, both in America and back home in Africa. Funding Sudanese-driven projects was something that I had been doing for ten years and could expertly contribute to. A generous bonus was the executive producer's fee, which helped me pay for my daughter's braces and send my college-age son to Africa to intern on the movie. Best of all, and beyond any of my dreamiest expectations, the producers kindly granted my husband and me *executive producer* credit together. The card read: "Deb & Bobby Newmyer."

A fantastic moment of gratitude for the man who had first championed the screenplay and the cause. He had lit the torch, and many of us had carried it onward.

Life doesn't always come full circle. But I promise you if you keep at it . . . with pluck and grit, there is a victory in your future.

"To whom much is given, much is required."
—Bill Gates, quoting John F Kennedy, quoting Luke 12:36

So What Are We Going to Tell Our Daughters (and Our Sons)?

A recent Harvard Business School study concluded that children are better off when their mom is a working role model.

Next year, a study might come out from Stanford that kids who are homeschooled do better in college. Or Google might determine that only children make better CEOs. BuzzFeed or Newsweek or PopSugar might be equally as convincing with another piece of study-based wisdom. The conventional wisdom is that as long as the mother is happy, and feels fulfilled, the kids will feel safe and become well-adjusted adults. That is probably true, but happiness is hard to measure, transfer, and teach.

Should we be specific and warn them away from corporate finance since Wall Street has the highest opt-out stats, and the worst reentry potential? Should we encourage them to be a nurse, since they only have to work twelve days a month? Or suggest academia, which has tremendous benefits and lengthy holidays? Or do we recommend civil service, which pays 80 percent of your income when you retire after thirty years? Do we not support them if they want to become an artist? Do we gift them the $15,000 on their thirtieth birthday so they can freeze their eggs and delay becoming a mother for a valuable career decade?

In every interview I asked:

- Did your mom work outside the house?
- How did your mom's work status inform yours?
- What mom quotes stand out the most?
- And what "Momisms" are now floating out of your mouth?
- So, then what occupational fields would you suggest to your daughter?

(http://qz.com/434056/working-moms-have-more-successful-daughters-and-more-caring-sons-harvard-business-school-study-says.)

Talking about life paths is always fascinating to me, but there were no consistent Dos or Don'ts among my samplings. Nor was there any secret occupational potion that allows Moms to *have it all*. The best personal and professional results came to women who were loudly encouraged by either their mothers or their fathers. The most prominent women were told they could "do anything they wanted to do!" . . . To "Go for It!". . . to "Never Give Up!". . . and those memorable shouts seemed to be the key to their success. Every prominent successful woman had one person—at least—who believed they could do it. Every successful story includes knowing how to ask for and use help.

Traditionally, women were directed into fields that could coincide with child-rearing schedules. Teaching gave you the summers off; after postmedical school, doctors got some flexibility into their schedule; Lawyers—if they didn't want to partner track—could work part-time for their hourly. Most of us were told to finish college and being a dancer won't pay.

During the muddle of child-rearing, mothers rarely have the bandwidth to be strategic. While your kids are under your roof, a primal immediacy takes over, and it's consuming enough to keep them healthy, to teach them how build kind friendships, and to steer them into a good college . . . and maybe win a few trophies along the way. I was always too busy untangling some trauma or planning a family trip to think too far ahead of their age range. While I was in the throes of parenting, I had no big-picture plan for my kids. I tried to help them find pleasure in hard work and give them coping skills for the fires that lay ahead. Mostly, mostly, I told them to find something they love to do. Some occupation that made them want to be awake and be productive. The harder they worked, the happier they would be. All I could say was go out and find the work that turns you on. Work hard, work smart, and the rest will follow.

Daily Do List

❑ Supported other Moms as they looked for new work.

❑ Remembered the politics workplace reform for women: flex-time, equal pay, and mentorship opportunities.

❑ Enjoyed my new gig and waited six months to complain.

❑ Encouraged my daughters and sons to find a job they could love.

❑ Personalized my own organizational habits with my own: daily to-do list, calendar system, tidying rituals.

CONCLUSION:
Nice Work . . . the World Needs You!

Writing a book is something I had never done before, and it turns out it's not easy. I am not a very fast writer, nor do I particularly like nonteamwork projects. I like an office. I like a telephone. I don't love researching and sitting at a computer, writing and rewriting. But my core friends kept encouraging me, and I truly believe that we are all better off when we are being productive, so I soldiered on. Hopefully, my positive exercises and coaxing will motivate other moms into their own new chapter.

However, the real reason this book took me so long to complete—nearly ten years—is that I got distracted by other jobs (professional and domestic). I did not have the time to do it all. I told myself I needed to get paid, which I did, and to carry on for the family. My deepest truth is that writing about being unemployed was often much harder than just getting a job. I avoided doing the spec work on the exact task that interested me the most. It was simply too frightening to not have an exact job title, so as soon as a I could find a "real" job, this book got put back in the file cabinet. It was especially hard to find the momentum to keep going at something that was this challenging and unknown for me. But eventually, I fought those fears, and I muddled through. And I can now say without feeling like it's an empty brag . . . Bravo, Deb. Your "Bravo" is right around the corner.

Along the windy, winding road of writing this book, I discovered many things about myself and my peers. I love listening to women tell their stories. I love being their bossy (but caring), common-sense girlfriend. And I have a knack for helping others traverse minefields that seem overwhelming from their own trenches.

More often than not, your path to productive happiness is right in front of you, barely hidden beneath the surface. But fear or inertia or lack of feeling supported is burying your potential success. More often than not, finding a rewarding career seems unreachable from the comfort of your kitchen in your well-worn yoga pants. However, if you follow the Steps of *Moms for Hire*—age, sex, and time out of the workplace aside—plenty of amazing and exciting careers lay ahead for the taking. You are not alone, and you are a valued member of a hidden resource of splendid and wise women. The very day-to-day tasks of motherhood you have endured and perfected have updated your résumé, so now let's go out and share your transferable talents with the needy world.

Becoming a *Mom for Hire* may have landed you in unexpected territories. Maybe the job you got is completely different from what you did prechildren. Or, after all this, the job offer came with a status and pay cut that hardly felt like a promotion. That's okay. Neither the good nor the bad times can last forever. *Meaningful work has got to be its own reward.* Keep aiming for the *best case scenario* in the job you've got. Commit your best angels to this career stop. Ambivalence won't make anyone happier. So decide to make the full leap in, and surprising glories will follow.

Do yourself a favor and don't expect perfection from your job. No job can be everything. It's rarely personal. Every person, every industry, every relationship grows and changes. And often, as things change, you will have to bend and weave, too. Wake up each morning, go out and do your best without expecting fabulous praise in return.

When it comes to the big-ticket items, remember that empowering other women is on the short list. Perhaps you can pass this book forward to another mother, or stow it on your own bookshelf for when your next job-hunting adventure comes along.

The family, the marriage, the office, the community, and the world are always better places when women are respected in the mix. The machinery of the world runs more smoothly when women bring their tool kit of maternal ingenuity and grit. It starts with you. And by prevailing as a *Mom for Hire*, you have contributed to a more flexible, more efficient, and kinder working world. Best thanks.

You got this, girlfriend.

WEB AND APP ASSISTS

" I don't always have the answers, but I always know who to ask. "
—July Malamud, single mother of three

It would have been nice if everything you needed to get your dream job was tucked between these covers. But I am not such an expert. I am, however, an expert in finding experts. Throughout the writing, I scouted out and leaned on many certified whizzes and mavens for specific advice. I have listed these pros, both as a shout-out to their dedicated work and as value-added as you work through the nitty-gritty steps. While I have vetted all these impressive sites, new experts are always emerging, and the more established ones are constantly upgrading. Hopefully, these supplemental homework helping sites and apps will inspire and prompt you onward.

Feel free to subscribe, bookmark, and/or simply appreciate the following deserving Apps and websites:

Step One: Get off the Couch
- *Unstuck.com* When you need a motivational push, *Unstuck* offers in-the-moment digital coaching. Very user-friendly (free) App option with action-oriented tips and tools, and provocative prompts. With an option for $49 advanced coaching conferences and programs.
- *LearnHowToBecome.org* Love this site. Helps you pinpoint your career interest and offers simple guides to every potential job path. Also, links you to UC Berkeley, Harvard University, and various Government and NGO career centers. It seems quite smart and kind. And it's free.
- *30/30 App Time Tracker* Download App in iTunes. The simpliest of the time tools, which lets you set tasks times and forces you to block out distractions.

Step Two: Get Organized

Look no further than the two greatest icons of organization:

- Julie Morgenstern, Organizing from the Inside-Out: The Foolproof System for Organizing your Home, Your Office and Your Life. www.juliemorgenstern.com/blog/
- Marie Kondo, The Life-Changing Magic of Tidying Up. www.tidyingup.com/ www.onekingslane.com/live-love-home/marie-kondo-book-declutter/

Both believe that messiness is a metaphor for unhappiness, and if you can declutter your sweaters, laptops, and suitcases, you will bring order to your life. Very clear and very systematic advice from either maven. Or if you still need help with your cluttered hoards, it might be time to hire a professional:

- www.napo.net National Association of Professional Organizers. Plug in your zip code and—like Angie's List—they'll direct you to the best organizer in your area.

Step Three: Get Unblocked

If you feel the need for a more intense rebooting of your work habits, there are plenty of transformational systems to choose from. For me, always rehabiting was my first step to a new chapter. It has been said that to break any habit (e.g., sweets, cigarettes, social media, messiness), you need a twenty-one-day cleanse to beat that viceful habit.

- *The Now Habit: A Strategic Program for Overcoming Procrastination and Enjoying Guilt-Free Play.* by Niel Fiore. Most people find this book "life-changing" and uniquely insightful. The easiest way to implant this system into your life is to listen to Niel's blog (http://www.neilfiore.com/) . . . or download as an audiobook . . . it's good car-speak for the whole family.
- Also, I found comforting fellowship in the words of Lisa Belkin's *Life's Work: Confessions of an Unbalanced Mom.*
- And I could count on a bit of a uplift with Ian Frazier's *The Cursing Mommy's Book of Days.*

Step Four: Get Looking

The two best (and most enviable for this author) websites for off-ramped Moms are:

- *iRelaunch.com* THE-RETURN-TO-WORK-EXPERTS. The most established resource for corporate, re-entry jobs. Offers encouraging support to female job hunters, even after decades away from the workforce. Plenty of free webinars once you subscribe, and constant notifications for more paid coaching, and more intense direction. A loud and respected shout-out to **iRelauch's** original authors, Carol Fishman Cohen and Vivian Steir Rabin, mega-career activist who founded the Mom-to-Job bandwagon over a decade ago with "Back on the Career Track: A Guide for Stay-at-Home Moms Who Want to Return to Work."

- **Apresgroup.com** Upscale and fast-growing site dedicated to woman reentry. Very classy and sleek website for the *au courant* Skimm set. Well worth joining for its smart and comfy advice. New York-based site, but quickly expanding nationally.
- Also, just give a quick look at your local **Craig's List Want Ad** listings; I have heard too many surprising success finds there to discount Craig's List as a rewarding job-search stop.

Step Five: Get Applying
Favorite Resume-Building Sites: none are perfect, but solid template starters:
- www.ResumeGenius.com
- www.LiveCareer.com

Favorite Job-Tracking Boards
- **LinkedIn.com** A must. If you only join one site, LinkedIn is the most comprehensive and most necessary.

LinkedIn is an absolute necessity. Browse and test a few others, and then, just join ONE more. It's better to be dedicated to a site and not paddle around in too many shallow ponds.
- **Glassdoor.com** Feels like the Yelp of jobsites, as they include easy access to employees and interviewers. Very helpful in the end phase.
- **ZipRecruiter.com** Offers specific criteria from employer and lets you know when your résumé has been opened and the progress of your application. Also, has an easy one-click application system and does not need you to write a new cover letter. Very efficient site, but less room for personalizing yourself.
- **The Muse.com** Specializes in start-ups and innovative companies and NGOs.
- **Indeed.com** National company with lots of offerings. But they come and go quickly.

(Disclaimer Note: I tried many many sites, and currently, the above are my personal favorites. However, I could not discover any independent studies regarding the yield and success rates of any of these job agencies. Anecdotal, they all seemed quite worthy, but I have no verifiable statistics on any of them. Hope you find one that is a good match for you.)

Step Six: Get Ready for your Interviews

- **www.interviewsuccessformula.com** Quickly expanding site that began as an insightful interview training course. And now covers most aspects of job-hunting. Subscribing and daily insights are free. However, Alan Carniol is such a dedicated spot-on job coach that paying for some of the webseminars is recommended.
- I love everything Alan Carniol says; he's so smart and conversational, and kind in his pushy clarity regarding how to get a job. If you only subscribe to one coaching site, make it Alan Carniol's, and a Daily Success Boost will arrive in your email every day.
- **www.Hireart.com** This site believes there are plenty of great employers looking for plenty of great workers, but there's a massive disconnect between the hirers and the hirees. HireArt recruits for many major national employers; however, a majority of the openings are entry-level. I highly recommend enrolling in this service, primarily for its innovative, videotaped Interviewing practice sessions.

Step Seven: Get Resilent and Keep Calling

Inspirational Podcast, Books, and Blogs of People who Prevailed.

- **ted.com/talks** Choose—by catergory—from 2,200 talks of articulate people who figure something out for themselves.
- **popsugar.com/moms** Of all the confectionary websites (*buzzfeed.com* for teens; **hellogiggles.com** for millennials), Pop Sugar is a guilty pleasure that is often informative and helpful.
- **TheLatestForMoms@popsugar.com**…Real Mom advice delivered daily, and at least once-a-week something fabulous.
- **theskimm.com** Female-driven global news delivered to your inbox every morning.
- **thefamilysaavy.com** My original partner on this book—Sarah Bowman—ended up focusing on a fabulous website designed to give you the shortcuts on everything your family "needs to know." By interest, by age, by neighborhood . . . this weekly blog is filled with great insight and activities.

Step Eight: Get Paid Properly

Tory Johnson—Workplace advocate, bestselling author, founder of **Woman for Hire and Spark & Hustle**—gives expert negotiating advice to deserving women.

- **womenforhire.com/negotiating_salary_benefits/negotiating_salary_101_ tactics_for_better_compensation/**

Most of these sites will impress you with enough inside-track information to hook you in: first one's free, and then they ask you to "Go Premium" or enroll in an online subscription course. Honestly, blogging takes time, and hard-working influencers should be paid, too. If someone's work is good, they should be compensated. No one should be asked give away their labor. So enjoy the trial sessions, and if you like the offer, pony up for the next level.

With immeasurable gratitude, I want to pass onward my eternal thanks to Richard N. Bolles, and his "WHAT COLOR IS YOUR PARACHUTE?" Bible for ALL career hunters. Since 1970, Mr. Bolles has been the foremost expert in Job Development and Happiness, and he has done more for national unemployment that any single individual. *Read his book!*

I encourage you to scan these sites; they are my reliable go-tos. And if you find a connection, keep going deeper into these wells. It's most effective and efficient to pick a site (or two) you really like and dive in with them. There is always a fine line between valuable, effective research and dillydallying in work avoidance. If you cast too wide of a net, you could spend your entire day procrastinating on the Internet and not tending to your own progressive exercises. As a job seeker, it is crucial to stay current with the outside world. In fact, I would schedule yourself some real time to scoot around your cybersites. Try not to get too sucked in, or you may end up with a carpal-syndrome mind like your teenagers, but a half an hour a day of budgeted time is essential and not indulgent.

ACKNOWLEDGMENTS

It would have been great if *Moms for Hire* was one of books that just "wrote itself." Hardly . . . For me, it was an arduous, uncharted trek from belief to bookshelf. While I always held fast to the vision of a chic guidebook tucked under the arm of an eager job hunter, I did not start out as an author nor as a particularly organized person. Soon, I discovered I was a slow writer and an even slower rewriter. While I tried to always be the cheerful, tireless worker, often I woke to my own doubting voice as I tried to avoid the kind eyes of my friends, who politely kept asking, "How's the book coming along?" (i.e., "Why's it taking you so long?") It took that village of fantastically bossy friends to keep supporting me with their clarity even when I lost mine. Somehow, I **never gave up,** and, finally, *Moms for Hire* exists as my newest career chapter.

My Third Shoulders (a.k.a My Coven of Bossy Girlfriends)

I shed many masturbatory tears writing this book, always hoping that crying would lead to the miracle of completion. But most of the time, the only way I could jump the hurdles was to find someone to listen to my venting and simply lend a hug. My core coven would always put down their own work, take on my phone call, and never once told me to shut up . . . I would have been sunk without their protective force fields, their clear vision of me, and their passion for twists and shouts: Michelle Kydd Lee, Katie McGrath, Lucy Fisher, Doug Wick, Ellen Horan, Tanya Lopez, Julie Miller, Sofi Newmyer, Sarah Jane Jelin, Lara Porzak, and the Sisters Wick. Wow to you all.

How Did SHE Do It?

I asked a lot of people to share their life stories. And while everyone seemed to enjoy the conversation, it is not easy to see the gist of their life paths retold as an anecdote. I have tremendous gratitude and respect for all those who spoke up and revealed themselves. Most of your stories ended up sliced into a specific exercise throughout *Moms for Hire,* either in actuality or disguised in a composite. Immeasurable thanks for crossing your barriers and offering an intimate piece of yourself as a role model. The world needs more wise women like each of you. I owe each of you an extra slice of gluten-free chocolate cake smothered in whipped coconut cream: Jamie Cole, Kathy Kennedy, Jocelyn Solomon, Nina Jacobson, Jen Bleakley, Cheryl Bloch, Deb Brierre, Yifat Orin, Paula Kaplan, Samantha Chapin, Monica Sarong, Ali Wentworth, Elizabeth English, Sophia Eitel McShea, Susan Sprung Kaiser, Fran Helm, Beth Kling, Maryann Rich, Amy Coleman, Jody Gerson, Nancy Tellem, Terri Press Marx, Terri Wakeman, Brooke Maille, Kaye P. Kramer, Kotra Blum, Lisa Licht, Bonnie Lee, Barbara Fisher, Deb Brierre, Roma Downey, Holly Jacobs, Jessica Lauter, Wendy Turner, Heidi Kenney, Maria Cuomo Cole, Kimberly Brooks, Cynthia Wick, Jessica Tuchinsky, Jane Buckingham, Romi Lasally, Phyllis Berger, Kimberly Brooks, Lisa Shue.

Official Experts and Heroines:
Mom advocates are not always the first girls picked at the dance, but hats off to all of you for shining a torch on all those unpaved highways. Some of you answered my calls, and others just lived their lives and—by example—gave tremendous impact to writing the book. Thank you. Thank you. And again Thank You: Lisa Belkin, Willow Bay, Stephanie Koontz, Sylvia Anne Hewlett, Maria Campbell, Nell Scovell, Maria Shriver, Arianna Huffington, Michelle Obama, Krista Smith, Ellie Sharef, Sheryl Sandberg.

Gratitude abounds to the early early readers. Your interest and brilliance gave me sustenance. Amy Iselin, Sarah Bowman, Pam Wick, Maggie Ribero. And when I needed professional guidance and fortitude, thanks for helping me unbundle things: Julie Wallach, Debra Oliver, Madeline Lodge, Amanda Marks. I could never have found my grammar, my command bar, or my cheerful stamina without the help of the grounded assistance of Sarah Burt, Madison Girifalco, and Gabby Zemer. And to the awesome ladies who carried the baton over the line: My tenacious agent, Laura Yorke, and my sage-yet-still-a millennial editor, Nicole Frail. And my patient, pitch-hitting editor Leah Zarra, who never let on to what a headache I had become.

Honestly, like every creative endeavor, I could not have prevailed without the infusion of caffeine, my ergonomic writing chair, and Amazon Prime's 1-click free delivery. I would be being ungrateful if I didn't also thank all my lovely distractions: That blooming magnolia tree outside my window onto Cashmere Street, those beckoning cyberportals and Candy Crush levels, my daughter's urgently forgotten basketball uniform, my Fritzi's nosey insistence that it's "time for a walk," and that lovely spur-of-the-moment lunch ask. Distractions are the spice of life. Thank you all.

Finally, forever thanks to my four remarkable children, who never allow me to be lonely or unloved. And for promising to support me as the decades dodder onward. My happiest of happiness comes from watching you thrive. I know you secretly appreciate my pushy insistences, my obsessive fear of losing things, and my spectacular dance floor moves. While you might still find me bewildering and even annoying, Sofi, Teddy, James, and Billi—you will always be my stabilizing ballast, my spiriting wind, and my lucky charms. Love you wicked and I live to make you proud.